Discovering spiritual gifts, helps identify your motivation from a supernatural perspective.

16 Spiritual Gifts Profile

Instructions: Every Christian is gifted with special motivation to bless them and benefit ministry. These motivational gifts are the specific ways we think, feel and act from a spiritual perspective. You can identify your spiritual gifts through this profile. Carefully follow these instructions —

Ask yourself how you feel about each one of the following statements. How true is each statement about you? Simply respond with the numerical rating as follows:

 • **5** — **Almost Always true;**
• **4** — **Often true;**
• **3** — **Sometimes true;**
• **2** — **Seldom true;**
• **1** — **Almost Never true.**

Avoid, as much as possible, a **3** (Sometimes) choice. Don't hesitate choosing **5** (Almost Always) or **1** (Almost Never). Your desire to be humble or not exaggerate may cause you to choose more moderate responses. This may affect your results. Try to be as honest as possible.

Example: "I love to hear evangelistic messages."

(Is this statement "**Almost Always**", "**Often**", "**Sometimes**", "**Seldom**" or "**Almost Never**" true about you? Try to choose the "**5, 4, 2** or **1.**" Avoid choosing the **3** "Sometimes.")

Place your numerical rating choice in the appropriate blank space before each statement provided on this and the next page. Then follow the instructions on the *Scoring and Plotting Instructions* page.

IMPORTANT: Be sure to avoid bleed-through from the Spiritual Gifts Questionnaire on the Uniquely You Questionnaire. Solution:

(1) Fold the profile under between the Historical Background and Uniquely You Questionnaire pages, so that the marks made on the preceding pages don't come through onto the Uniquely You Questionnaire page, or

(2) Give everyone a blank piece of paper to place on top of the Uniquely You Questionnaire page as a buffer.

1. ___ I tend to motivate others to get involved.

2. ___ I like starting new churches from scratch.

3. ___ I can tell when people are insincere.

4. ___ I love to hear messages about salvation.

5. ___ Teaching the facts without practical application is really lacking.

6. ___ God has given me unusual assurances of His control.

7. ___ People misunderstand my financial interests.

8. ___ I love to provide my home as a haven or meeting place.

9 ___ My study of the Scriptures gives me unique knowledge.

10. ___ I would rather be THE leader, than just one of the leaders.

11. ___ I tend to be super sensitive to sad stories.

12. ___ I tend to be irritated when people sin.

13. ___ I tend to get frustrated when the church is not growing.

14. ___ I will do the little things no one else wants to do.

15. ___ Education is very important to me.

16. ___ I tend to make wise decisions and choices.

17. ___ I can do a lot of things at once.

18. ___ I would be willing to move elsewhere to start a church.

19. ___ I can tell when others teach or share inaccurate info.

20. ___ Leading people to Christ is so exciting.

21. ___ I like to share practical steps of action.

22. ___ I always believe and see how God works in our lives.

23. ___ I tend to give money freely where needed most.

24. ___ I tend to make total strangers feel at home.

25. ___ I have an ability to acquire Bible facts and principles.

26. ___ I feel frustrated when it looks like no one is in charge

27. ___ I spend a lot of time helping others feel better.

28. ___ I discern something is evil, before others do.

29. ___ I enjoy leading discipleship type Bible studies.

30. ___ I prefer serving others, rather than being served.

31. ___ Preparation to speak or teach is absolutely necessary.

32. ___ I seem to be able to help others make right decisions.

33. ___ I do my best work under pressure.

34. ___ I adapt well to other cultures and groups.

35. ___ I am able to differentiate between true and false needs.

36. ___ I am very concerned about lost souls.

37. ___ I teach topical, rather than verse-by-verse lessons.

38. ___ Trusting God for the impossible comes easy to me.

39. ___ I tend to make wise investments.

40. ___ I like to invite people in need to stay in my home.

41. ___ I learn and remember biblical truth easily.

42. ___ I know where I'm headed and am driven to bring others.

43. ___ I can't say, "No" to legitimate needs.

44. ___ I research to share truth, rather than just to study.

45. ___ I seem to look for spiritual lessons in whatever happens.

46. ___ Solving problems is my main concern.

47. ___ I like to explain why something is true.

48. ___ I easily see the difference between truth and error.

49. ___ I tend to take charge when no one else does.

50. ___ I would rather start a new church, than anything else.

51. ___ I am able to read between the lines of what others say.

52. ___ Worldwide evangelism really excites me.

53. ___ I tend to use biblical illustrations to explain things.

54. ___ I'm comfortable around people who like to pray a lot.

55. ___ Financial accountability is extremely important.

56. ___ I look for opportunities to use my home to help others.

Instructions:

Ask yourself how you feel about each statement.
How true is each statement about you?
Respond with the numerical rating as follows:

- 5 — Almost Always;
- 4 — Often;
- 3 — Sometimes;
- 2 — Seldom;
- 1 — Almost Never.

(Avoid the "3 — Sometimes" choice, as much as possible.)

57. ___ I study the Bible to gain more knowledge about things.

58. ___ I often volunteer to take charge of difficult projects.

59. ___ Some people think I'm too sensitive.

60. ___ I like to proclaim truth I have received from God.

61. ___ I often seek to help individuals grow in Christ.

62. ___ I tend to take on a lot of opportunities to serve people.

63. ___ It bothers me to hear incorrect statements and teaching.

64. ___ People often seek me out for wise advice.

65. ___ I like impossible challenges.

66. ___ I get real excited about new mission works worldwide.

67. ___ I am able to easily detect unspiritual things.

68. ___ I enjoy asking people to make decisions for Christ.

69. ___ I really enjoy encouraging others.

70. ___ I want people to pray more and increase their faith.

71. ___ I tend to discern true financial needs.

72. ___ My home is always open to anyone or for any group.

73. ___ I take serious the command to "increase in knowledge."

74. ___ I am driven to move forward even when others aren't.

75. ___ When others hurt, I feel compelled to help.

76. ___ I can be stubborn and difficult to convince.

77. ___ I prefer being a spiritual leader.

78. ___ I don't like being up-front or leading a group.

79. ___ I tend to prepare too much material.

80. ___ I like to solve problems through the wisdom of the Word.

81. ___ I like to organize people to accomplish great tasks.

82. ___ I prefer serving in a cross-cultural ministry.

83. ___ I am a good judge of what is good and evil.

84. ___ I like to lead people to Christ with my testimony.

85. ___ Practical application is what teaching is all about.

86. ___ I have strong assurances that God answers prayer.

87. ___ I like to take care of financial needs in a timely manner.

88. ___ A neat home is not as important as its availability.

89. ___ I often feel compelled to study and learn biblical truth.

90. ___ People often say that I am a good leader.

91. ___ I try to come across as loving and caring.

92. ___ I tend to know why people do what they do.

93. ___ Leading groups to spiritual maturity is most appealing.

94. ___ I tend to do much more than I'm told to do.

95. ___ Studying the Scriptures is my passion.

96. ___ I believe wisdom is more important than faith or knowledge.

97. ___ I would rather speak out, than just let something pass.

98. ___ I am attracted to ministries that start new churches.

99. ___ People say that I often have just the right advice.

100. ___ I can share the gospel with total strangers.

101. ___ I often feel compelled to share advice.

102. ___ I tend to judge people by how much faith they have.

103. ___ I'm concerned about meeting financial/physical needs.

104. ___ I feel church members need to be more hospitable.

105. ___ I like to learn things most people don't know.

106. ___ It bothers me when people sit around and do nothing.

107. ___ I tend to volunteer to help the less fortunate.

108. ___ Confronting someone with sin in their life is not hard.

109. ___ People seek me out to become spiritually stronger.

110. ___ Working behind the scenes gives me much pleasure.

111. ___ I search for new insights as I study.

112. ___ People are often amazed at how much knowledge I have.

113. ___ I delegate responsibilities to accomplish tasks.

114. ___ I believe an apostle today is God's pioneer and authority.

115. ___ I seem to have a unique discernment in many areas.

116. ___ Sharing my faith is most important to me.

117. ___ I really enjoy counseling others.

118. ___ People say I have a tremendous amount of faith.

119. ___ Being slothful, "lazy" in business is a sin.

120. ___ I believe hospitality is one of the most important things.

121. ___ I believe having great knowledge is very important.

122. ___ Opposition doesn't bother me as much as just sitting still.

123. ___ I'm very concerned about how a person feels.

124. ___ People say I'm too protective and strict with others.

125. ___ I like to help others to get involved in ministry.

126. ___ I would rather do a job myself, rather than delegate it.

127. ___ Digging deep into the Word of God is a priority in life.

128. ___ People often say I demonstrate lots of unusual wisdom.

Once you have completed the questionnaire, fold this page in half along the dotted line (fold this side under the left side), then follow Scoring Instructions ❶ on the exposed part of the following Spiritual Gifts Graph page.

4

❶ Scoring Instructions

Be sure to first rate your response to each choice from the separate Spiritual Gifts questionnaire. Record your choice (5, 4, 3, 2, or 1) in the appropriate numbered question box. Total each column. Then follow *Plotting Instructions* ❷.

Scoring Example: ✍

1	2	3	4
4	5	1	2

❷ Plotting Instructions

To plot your Spiritual Gifts Graph, first complete the *Scoring Instructions* at ❶.

Then use the totals from your Numerical Ratings Chart to plot your graph below. Find the appropriate letter **A, B, C, D, E, F, G, H, I, J, K, L, M, N, O,** or **P** in the Spiritual Gifts Graph below and circle the number of the total under each letter. Notice Plotting Example.

Numerical Ratings Chart

✍

1	2	3	4	5	6	7	8	9	10	11	12	13	14	15	16
17	18	19	20	21	22	23	24	25	26	27	28	29	30	31	32
33	34	35	36	37	38	39	40	41	42	43	44	45	46	47	48
49	50	51	52	53	54	55	56	57	58	59	60	61	62	63	64
65	66	67	68	69	70	71	72	73	74	75	76	77	78	79	80
81	82	83	84	85	86	87	88	89	90	91	92	93	94	95	96
97	98	99	100	101	102	103	104	105	106	107	108	109	110	111	112
113	114	115	116	117	118	119	120	121	122	123	124	125	126	127	128
A	**B**	**C**	**D**	**E**	**F**	**G**	**H**	**I**	**J**	**K**	**L**	**M**	**N**	**O**	**P**

Total:

✍

Total: | **A** 32 | **B** 18 |

Plotting Example (A B columns):

```
        A    B
       40   40
       39   39
       38   38
       37   37
       36   36
       35   35
       34   34
       33   33
      (32)  32
       31   31
       30   30
       29   29
       28   28
       27   27
       26   26
       25   25
       24   24
       23   23
       22   22
       21   21
       20   20
       19   19
       18  (18)
       17   17
       16   16
       15   15
       14   14
       13   13
       12   12
       11   11
       10   10
        9    9
        8    8
```

Your Spiritual Gifts Graph

Administ / Ruling	Apostleship/ Pioneer.	Discernment	Evangelism	Encouraging / Exhort	Faith	Giving	Hospitality	Knowledge	Leadership	Showing Mercy	Prophecy/ Perceiving	Pastor / Shepherding	Serving / Ministry	Teaching	Wisdom
A	**B**	**C**	**D**	**E**	**F**	**G**	**H**	**I**	**J**	**K**	**L**	**M**	**N**	**O**	**P**
40	40	40	40	40	40	40	40	40	40	40	40	40	40	40	40
39	39	39	39	39	39	39	39	39	39	39	39	39	39	39	39
38	38	38	38	38	38	38	38	38	38	38	38	38	38	38	38
37	37	37	37	37	37	37	37	37	37	37	37	37	37	37	37
36	36	36	36	36	36	36	36	36	36	36	36	36	36	36	36
35	35	35	35	35	35	35	35	35	35	35	35	35	35	35	35
34	34	34	34	34	34	34	34	34	34	34	34	34	34	34	34
33	33	33	33	33	33	33	33	33	33	33	33	33	33	33	33
32	32	32	32	32	32	32	32	32	32	32	32	32	32	32	32
31	31	31	31	31	31	31	31	31	31	31	31	31	31	31	31
30	30	30	30	30	30	30	30	30	30	30	30	30	30	30	30
29	29	29	29	29	29	29	29	29	29	29	29	29	29	29	29
28	28	28	28	28	28	28	28	28	28	28	28	28	28	28	28
27	27	27	27	27	27	27	27	27	27	27	27	27	27	27	27
26	26	26	26	26	26	26	26	26	26	26	26	26	26	26	26
25	25	25	25	25	25	25	25	25	25	25	25	25	25	25	25
24	24	24	24	24	24	24	24	24	24	24	24	24	24	24	24
23	23	23	23	23	23	23	23	23	23	23	23	23	23	23	23
22	22	22	22	22	22	22	22	22	22	22	22	22	22	22	22
21	21	21	21	21	21	21	21	21	21	21	21	21	21	21	21
20	20	20	20	20	20	20	20	20	20	20	20	20	20	20	20
19	19	19	19	19	19	19	19	19	19	19	19	19	19	19	19
18	18	18	18	18	18	18	18	18	18	18	18	18	18	18	18
17	17	17	17	17	17	17	17	17	17	17	17	17	17	17	17
16	16	16	16	16	16	16	16	16	16	16	16	16	16	16	16
15	15	15	15	15	15	15	15	15	15	15	15	15	15	15	15
14	14	14	14	14	14	14	14	14	14	14	14	14	14	14	14
13	13	13	13	13	13	13	13	13	13	13	13	13	13	13	13
12	12	12	12	12	12	12	12	12	12	12	12	12	12	12	12
11	11	11	11	11	11	11	11	11	11	11	11	11	11	11	11
10	10	10	10	10	10	10	10	10	10	10	10	10	10	10	10
9	9	9	9	9	9	9	9	9	9	9	9	9	9	9	9
8	8	8	8	8	8	8	8	8	8	8	8	8	8	8	8

❸

Reading Your Graph:

To determine which gifts are most like you, connect the circles. Notice which gifts are most intense. The higher on the profile, the more intensely that gift describes you. Also notice your next highest and lowest plotting points to learn more about your overall gift tendencies.

Spiritual Gifts Descriptions

Spiritual Gifts are supernatural motivations given to every believer. Everyone doesn't receive the same gift. Just as many parts of the human body work together as one, so Spiritual Gifts are given to the Body of Christ to serve as one.

Their purpose is to encourage and mature Christians for more effective ministry. This profile focuses on sixteen spiritual gifts. These sixteen gifts are featured based upon their functional and practical use.

Administration / Ruling —

The Gift of Administration / Ruling is seen in those who either like to organize or delegate to others. Compelled by a strong sense of duty, they like to find things for people to do. Unlike the Gift of Ministry, the Gift of Administration / Ruling focuses on team participation. They see the big picture and work to keep everyone on track. Not always personally organized, they prefer delegating tasks. They simply like to evaluate what needs to be done, then design systems or give responsibilities to those who can get the job done. They are gifted to forge forward as a group.

In a word: Initiator
Overuse: Expects too much
Goal: Lead by example, not manipulation
Scripture: Romans 12:8; 1 Corinthans 12:28; Acts 6:1-7

Apostleship / Pioneering —

Unlike Apostles of old, who actually saw the Lord and spread the Word from place to place, Apostles today have a clear vision to start new ministries where others may not. They make great church planters and strong leaders. Apostles today have a self / spirited appointed calling to reach out where others may never dare. They demonstrate tremendous abilities in influencing others to follow. They also have contagious and industrious enthusiasm to cross cultural, geographical, and economic boundaries for Christ. Apostles today are often used by God as anointed authorities in their region and ministry.

In a word: Pioneer / Visionary
Overuse: Pushes too hard / Too much authority
Goal: Build deeper and stronger
Scripture: Ephesians 4:7,11; 1 Cor. 9:1-2; Gal. 2:8-10; 1 Cor. 12:28-29

Discernment —

The Gift of Discernment is evident in those who have unusual ability to see through a lot of confusion and pin point problems and solutions. They are concerned about right and wrong. They tend to listen well and hear the little and seemingly insignificant things that shed light on a specific need. Those with the Gift of Discernment are often more serious. They distinquish between good and evil, truth and error. They like to ask questions and then give advise. They often relate problems to the violation of biblical principles. They feel strongly about obeying truth and living by the Word of God.

In a word: Listeners / Perceiver
Overuse: Too critical or too quick to share
Goal: Get more information before responding
Scripture: 1 Corinthans 12:7,10b; 1 Corinthans 2:14

Encouraging / Exhorting —

Christians with the Gift of Encouraging find themselves exhorting others. They are compelled to give advice. As counselors, they seem to often have steps of action. While Prophets declare truth and Teachers clarify truth, Encouragers / Exhorters like to tell you what to do with truth. They bless others with a strong sense of concern. Often looking to encourage others, they are sought out as counselors. People find Encouragers friendly, understanding and practical. They enjoy using their communication skills to share specific insights.

In a word: Encourager
Overuse: Talks too much
Goal: Apply truth, don't create expectations
Scripture: Romans 12:6,8; Acts 11:23-24; Hebrews 10:24-25

Evangelism —

Christians with the Gift of Evangelism feel compelled to win souls. They seem to have the ability to communicate the gospel very effectively. Their concern for witnessing to a lost and dying world is evident. They desire to be involved in ministries to reach people for Christ. The Gift of Evangelism motivates them to want nearly every message they hear to include the gospel and an invitation to trust Christ. Missions and outreach are important to them. Always being ready to give an answer to every person is their goal. Conversations seem to often turn toward eternal values. The worth of souls and the task of evangelism are most important to the Evangelist's motivation.

In a word: Dynamic
Overuse: Zeal
Goal: Build disciples, not statistics
Scripture: Ephesians 4:7,11; Acts 8:26-40; Luke 19:1-10

Faith —

The Gift of Faith is often found in those with the obvious ability to trust God in the most adverse circumstances. Every Christian has a measure of saving faith, but those with the Gift of Faith have a deeper dependence upon God and His Word. "Faith comes by hearing and hearing by the Word of God," is often their favorite Bible verse. The Gift of Faith is seen in those who believe strongly in the presence and power of God. They tend to stretch the faith and commitments of others. They encourage others to act upon their faith and challenge everyone to increase their faith.

In a word: Optimist
Overuse: Overly trusting and often proud of their faith
Goal: Combine faith with works / Learn to be patient with others
Scripture: 1 Corinthans 12:7,9; Mattew 8:5-16; Hebrews 11:1

Giving —

Givers tend to be seriously concerned about financial matters. The Gift of Giving also involves the "gift of getting." Givers are sensitive to how money is spent and saved. Those with the Gift of Giving don't always give to the wheel that squeaks the loudest, but to the wheel that truly needs the most grease. Givers have unique financial insights. They serve especially well on boards responsible for maintaining budgets. They tend to be conscientious and conservative. The Gift of Giving may not be always evident, but a genuine interest in wise stewardship will be.

In a word: Steward
Overuse: The power of money
Goal: Sincere stewardship, not financial harassment
Scripture: Romans 12:6,8b; Acts 4:32-35; 2 Corinthians 9:7-8

Hospitality —

The Gift of Hospitality is that special interest in opening one's home for food and fellowship, or to just provide a place to stay for someone in need. Those with the Gift of Hospitality seem to always be ready and willing to invite guests over or offer their home for a place to meet for any occasion. They love to provide refreshments or prepare meals for individuals or groups. They seldom show irritation over last minute requests to have someone over or to host a group. They tirelessly serve to make people comfortable and encouraged.

In a word: Sociable
Overuse: Take on too much / Get worn out
Goal: Provide fellowship without sacrificing family time
Scripture: 1 Peter 4:9-10; Acts 16:13-15; Luke 14:12-14

To identify your Spiritual Gifts, follow the **Scoring Instructions ❶** on the questionnaire page. Once you have plotted your Spiritual Gifts Graph you should study these pages with their brief summaries of all the gifts.

These descriptions are simple overviews of the Spiritual Gifts listed in Romans 12:3-8, Ephesians 4:11-12, 1 Corinthians 12:8-28, and 1 Corinthians 14:1-3. Read each one, along with reviewing the results of your Spiritual Gifts Profile to identify your specific spiritual motivations.

There are many spiritual gifts referred to in the Scriptures. We are only looking at those that help us "fit" and relate best in ministry. There are also various manifestations of the gifts. This profile does not deal with any of the manifestations, but rather the motivations and ministries of sixteen specific gifts.

This tool is not intended to be as theological, as it is to be practical and pragmatic. The main purpose of discovering your spiritual gifts is to exercise and enjoy your giftedness for God's glory and to grow as a Christian.

Knowledge —

The Gift of Knowledge is a supernatural revelation of certain facts in the mind of God, which gives instant and specific information that one would have no other way of knowing, except from God. This is not an amplification of human knowledge, nor is it a gift of just knowing a lot of things. It is the ability to receive specific truth from the Word of God. Sometimes they may overwhelm others and bring more attention to their Word of Knowledge, rather than the purpose of sharing what God has revealed to them.

In a word: Divine Insights
Overuse: Make others feel inferior or ignorant
Goal: Change lives, rather than impress others
Scripture: 1 Corinthans 12:7-8; 8:1b-2

Prophecy / Perceiving—

Prophets today are not exactly like prophets of old. Old Testament Prophets spoke the literal Word of God. Today people with the Gift of Prophecy seem to have the same seriousness and straight forward attitude toward truth. They like to share truth, regardless of what anyone thinks. Prophets today are motivated to confront anyone with what they believe is right. When controlled by the Holy Spirit, the Gift of Prophecy is a powerful tool to reprove, rebuke and exhort others. Prophets often find themselves pointing the way, declaring specific truth or standing up for something significant.

In a word: Bold
Overuse: Fighter
Goal: Declare truth, don't divide Christians
Scripture: Ephesians. 4:7,11; 1 Corinthians 14:1,3; 2 Peter 1:19-21

Leadership —

The Gift of Leadership, much like the Gift of Administration / Ruling, is evident in those who demonstrate an unusual ability to influence others. They seem to have an independent determination to challenge and direct others toward a specific goal. They stand out and take stands. Those with the Gift of Leadership tend to be multi-talented excelling with their people and tasks skills. Often result-oriented and driven, they need to guard their strengths. They also need to be more sensitive and patient with those who don't respond as well or positive as they. They are great motivators.

In a word: Dreamer
Overuse: Too demanding and impatient
Goal: Lead by example and willingness to be a servant
Scripture: Romans 12:6,8c; John 13:13-17; Hebrews 13:17

Serving / Ministry / Helps —

When you think of Christians who serve faithfully behind the scenes, you think of those with the Gift of Serving / Ministry / Helps. They are interested in blessing others to serve the Lord. They love to help others. Motivated by a strong sense of need, they feel like "someone has to do it." Caring and concerned for others, they find themselves doing what no one else likes to do. They tend to do whatever called for. Flexible, they adapt to many challenges. They simply enjoy helping others and meeting needs. Often truly selfless, those with this gift like to be involved.

In a word: Selfless
Overuse: Takes on too much
Goal: Be a servant, not a martyr
Scripture: 1 Corinthians . 12:28; Act. 6:1-3; Romans 16:1-2

Mercy —

Christians with the Gift of Showing Mercy demonstrates genuine sensitivity to suffering. They are compelled to help people reduce pain. They are concerned more with the person, than the reason for the suffering. Focusing on the feelings of those who hurt, Showers of Mercy desire to minister by "being there" when people really need them. Sympathizing and/or empathizing are their specialties. While others may care more about why, what, when or how, those with the Showing Mercy are interested in "who" needs tender loving care.

In a word: Caring
Overuse: Too sensitive
Goal: Wise insights, not foolish responses
Scripture: Romans 12:6,8d; Matthew 5:7

Teaching —

Christians with the Gift of Teaching prefer explaining why things are true. While the prophet declares truth, the teacher explains the reasons why it is true. Interested in research, those with the Gift of Teaching like to dig into seemingly insignificant details. They enjoy presenting what they discover. Often negligent of the needs of others, they press toward a deeper understanding. They love to study. Searching patiently and persistently, they may miss the obvious. They stretch the limits of learning, setting high standards of education.

In a word: In-depth
Overuse: Digs too deep
Goal: Reveal truth, don't exhaust it
Scripture: Romans 12:6,7b; Colossians 3:16; James. 3:1; 2; 2 Timothy2:2

Pastor / Shepherding —

The Gift of Pastor / Shepherding is obvious in those who really enjoy leading others in serving the Lord. Unlike the Gift of Ministry / Serving /Helps, this gift involves the motivation to lead. Pastor / Shepherds are compelled to encourage others to work together for the body's sake. Influencing others to work together is important. Stressing a need for team participation, they emphasize harmony. Untrained lay-people can also have the Gift of Pastor / Shepherding. They see their service as one of maturing others. With a motivation to unite the ministry, they feel strong about spiritual health.

In a word: Discipler / Leader
Overuse: Takes Advantage of Others' Trust
Goal: Strong leadership, not manipulating the flock
Scripture: Ephesians 4:11; 1 Peter 5:2-4

Wisdom —

The Gift of Wisdom is the unique ability to use knowledge in a practical way. Those with this gift like to combine what they know with a serious reverence of God in order to influence others. They sometimes battle with pride and an attitude of superiority. They need to be consistently humble and exhibit a sense of quietness and slowness before responding. Those with the Gift of Wisdom are often given some kind of adversity to stay in tune with God and His Word. Otherwise, those with this gift will tend to be puffed up. They make great counselors and give tremendous advice. Therefore, they need to stay in constant prayer, asking God for His wisdom.

In a word: Perceptive
Overuse: Speak down to people
Goal: Consistently trust and ask God for wisdom
Scripture: 1 Corinthians 12:7-8; James 3:13-18

7

Historical Background

The Four Temperament Model of Human Behavior is attributed to Hippocrates, the father of modern medicine. His scientific research and brilliant observations are universally accepted. Contrary to what critics claim, the Four Temperaments did not hatch from archaic pagan greek philosophy, but rather the scientific process that made Hippocrates the respected physician of his day.

The DISC Model of Human Behavior was first introduced by William Marston in 1928 through his book, The Emotions Of Normal People. Marston took Hippocrates' Greek titles and assigned simple and single D, I, S, and C letters to each. Though there are now many titles to various models, they all have roots from the same basic four temperaments discovered 400 B.C.

Dr. John Geier, Chairman of the Human Behavior Science Department at the University of Minnesota designed the first paper assessment that identified a person's DISC personality type from a business and personal perspective in 1977.

After studying under Dr. Geier with Performax Systems and Dr. Frank Wichern, Staff Psychologist at Dallas Theological Seminary, Dr. Mels Carbonell designed the first-of-their-kind combination personality and faith-based profiles. With over 1 million profiles now in print in several different languages, Uniquely You Resources are one of the most respected and popular profiles available for businesses, personal use, and faith-based organizations.

Understanding the four-quadrant model of basic human behavior often explains why people do what they do. These insights can make the difference between right and wrong responses, and the best or worst behavior in any situation.

The profile is not a psychological analysis. It is not designed to deal with serious emotional problems. It can help with simple insights into basic human behavior motivations. For more in-depth needs, we recommend you seek "professional" counseling.

To receive maximum effectiveness, be sure to complete your personality profile. There are so many insights to learn!

Continue on the following pages to complete
your *Uniquely You Questionnaire.*

❶ *Uniquely You Questionnaire*

FOCUS: _____ Home OR _____ Work; DATE_____

Name _____ ☐ Male; ☐ Female; ORGANIZATION _____

❷ INSTRUCTIONS: Notice each group of words below. For each group, ask yourself which words are **MOST** and which words are **LEAST** like you. Do not choose what you want to be or what you want others to think you are, but what you really are under pressure. Fill in **ONLY ONE** box in the "**M**" column **MOST** like you and fill in **ONLY** one box in the "**L**" column **LEAST** like you. All of the words or none of them may or may not describe you, but choose **ONLY ONE** group of words. Notice in the "Example" how **ONLY ONE** box is filled in under the "**M**" and "**L**" columns.

M L   Example:
- ☒ ☐ Kind, Nice, Caring
- ☐ ☐ Proper, Formal
- ☐ ☒ Demanding, Asserting
- ☐ ☐ Outgoing, Active

M L

1. ☐ ☐ Kind, Nice, Caring
2. ☐ ☐ Proper, Formal
3. ☐ ☐ Demanding, Asserting
4. ☐ ☐ Outgoing, Active

5. ☐ ☐ Playful, Fun-loving
6. ☐ ☐ Firm, Strong
7. ☐ ☐ Law-abiding, Conscientious
8. ☐ ☐ Gentle, Soft, Humble

9. ☐ ☐ Bold, Daring
10. ☐ ☐ Delightful, Pleasant
11. ☐ ☐ Loyal, True Blue
12. ☐ ☐ Calculating, Analytical

13. ☐ ☐ Conservative, Inflexible
14. ☐ ☐ Trusting, Gullible, Open
15. ☐ ☐ Peaceful, Calm
16. ☐ ☐ Convinced, Cocky

17. ☐ ☐ Decisive, Sure, Certain
18. ☐ ☐ Friendly, Cordial, Popular
19. ☐ ☐ Careful, Cautious
20. ☐ ☐ Obedient, Submissive

21. ☐ ☐ Promoting, Encouraging
22. ☐ ☐ Straight, Conforming
23. ☐ ☐ Risk-taking, Courageous
24. ☐ ☐ Pleasing, Good-natured

25. ☐ ☐ Considerate, Thoughtful
26. ☐ ☐ Forceful, Strong-willed
27. ☐ ☐ Hyper, Energetic
28. ☐ ☐ Perfectionist, Precise

29. ☐ ☐ Contented, Satisfied
30. ☐ ☐ Compliant, Goes by book
31. ☐ ☐ Brave, Adventurous
32. ☐ ☐ Enthusiastic, Influencing

M L

33. ☐ ☐ Smooth talker, Articulate
34. ☐ ☐ Loving, Sincere, Honest
35. ☐ ☐ Persistent, Restless, Relentless
36. ☐ ☐ Right, Correct

37. ☐ ☐ Positive, Optimistic
38. ☐ ☐ Entertaining, Clowning
39. ☐ ☐ Shy, Mild
40. ☐ ☐ Competent, Does Right

41. ☐ ☐ Contemplative, Thinker
42. ☐ ☐ Diplomatic, Peacemaking
43. ☐ ☐ Admirable, Elegant
44. ☐ ☐ Winner, Competitive

45. ☐ ☐ Joyful, Jovial
46. ☐ ☐ Flexible, Adaptable, Agreeable
47. ☐ ☐ Ambitious, Goes for it
48. ☐ ☐ Deep, Intense

49. ☐ ☐ Steady, Dependable
50. ☐ ☐ Talkative, Verbal
51. ☐ ☐ Challenging, Motivating
52. ☐ ☐ Accurate, Exact

53. ☐ ☐ Stable, Balanced
54. ☐ ☐ Confident, Self-reliant
55. ☐ ☐ Perceptive, Sees clearly
56. ☐ ☐ Animated, Expressive

57. ☐ ☐ Controlling, Taking charge
58. ☐ ☐ Merciful, Sensitive
59. ☐ ☐ Pondering, Wondering
60. ☐ ☐ Persuading, Convincing

61. ☐ ☐ Sociable, Interactive
62. ☐ ☐ Serious, Unwavering
63. ☐ ☐ Sweet, Tender, Compassionate
64. ☐ ☐ Guarded, Masked, Protective

M L

65. ☐ ☐ Powerful, Unconquerable
66. ☐ ☐ Merry, Cheerful
67. ☐ ☐ Generous, Giving
68. ☐ ☐ Preparing, Researching

69. ☐ ☐ Timid, Soft-spoken
70. ☐ ☐ Systematic, Follows plan
71. ☐ ☐ Industrious, Hard working
72. ☐ ☐ Smiling, Happy

73. ☐ ☐ Inquisitive, Questioning
74. ☐ ☐ Tolerant, Patient
75. ☐ ☐ Driving, Determined
76. ☐ ☐ Dynamic, Impressing

77. ☐ ☐ Serving, Sacrificing
78. ☐ ☐ Sharp, Appealing
79. ☐ ☐ Direct, To the point
80. ☐ ☐ Original, Creative

81. ☐ ☐ Peppy, Playful
82. ☐ ☐ Devoted, Dedicated
83. ☐ ☐ Courteous, Polite
84. ☐ ☐ Strict, Unbending

85. ☐ ☐ Outspoken, Opinionated
86. ☐ ☐ Inducing, Charming
87. ☐ ☐ Inventive, Imaginative
88. ☐ ☐ Hospitable, Enjoys company

89. ☐ ☐ Zealous, Eager
90. ☐ ☐ Quiet, Reserved
91. ☐ ☐ Organized, Orderly
92. ☐ ☐ Exciting, Spirited

93. ☐ ☐ Faithful, Consistent
94. ☐ ☐ Responsive, Reacting
95. ☐ ☐ Helpful, Assisting
96. ☐ ☐ Bottom line, Straight-forward

Once you have completed your choices on this page, go to the **❹ Markings Sheet** *page and follow the instructions.*

9

③Counting Instructions:

• First, notice the carbon marks in the boxes on the following ❹*Markings Sheet*. The "M" boxes have D, I, S, C, and B letters to their left and the "L" boxes have D, I, S, C, and B letters to their right. Transfer the letters marked in the specific "M" and "L" boxes on the following ❹*Markings Sheet* to the "M" and "L" blank spaces to the ❺ right of each group of boxes.

• Count all the "D"s marked and transferred under the three "M" columns on the following ❹*Markings Sheet* page. Be sure to count all "D"s with a carbon mark filled in and transferred only in the "M" columns. Record the total "D"s counted in the ❻*TOTAL BOXES* below. Then count all the "I"s marked and transferred under the three "M" columns. Record the total "I"s counted in the ❻*TOTAL BOXES*. Do the same with the total "S"s, "C"s, and "B"s spaces marked and transferred on the following ❹*Markings Sheet* page.

• Count all the "D"s marked and transferred under the three "L" columns. Be sure to count all the "D"s with a carbon mark filled in and transferred only in the "L" columns. Record the total "D"s counted in the ❻*TOTAL BOXES* below. Then count all the "I"s marked and transferred under the three "L" columns. Record the total "I"s counted in the ❻*TOTAL BOXES*. Do the same with the total "S"s, "C"s, and "B"s spaces marked and transferred.

• Add the total number of "D"s, "I"s, "S"s, "C"s, and "B"s spaces counted in the ❻ *TOTAL BOXES* below. It should total 24. Be sure to count the "B" spaces under the three "M" columns before trying to total 24. Do the same with the three "L" columns before trying to total 24. If it doesn't add up to 24, recount and try putting a check mark by each one as you count it.

❻ *TOTAL BOXES*

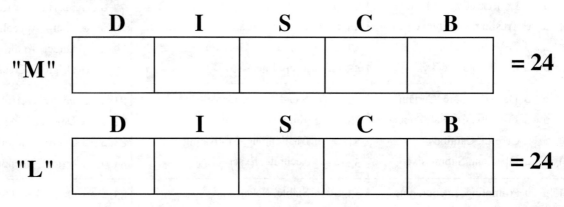

"M"   D   I   S   C   B   = 24

"L"   D   I   S   C   B   = 24

Once you have recorded the total number of "D"s, "I"s, "S"s, and "C"s in your ❻TOTAL BOXES above, use those specific numbers to plot ❼ Graphs 1 and 2 on the Plotting Instructions page.

Notice "M" numbers above should be plotted on the "M" (Graph 1) series of boxes. "L" numbers above should be plotted on the "L"❼ (Graph 2) on the Plotting Instructions page.

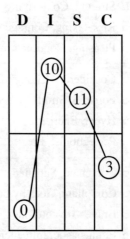

Example: **TOTAL BOXES**

D	I	S	C
0	10	11	3

❹ MARKINGS SHEET

To help in counting the total Most and Least D's, I's, S's, and C's, you should write your choice to the side of each group of letters marked. First, record the letters marked in the specific **M** and **L** boxes to the **M and L** ❺ blank spaces to the right of each group of boxes, then continue with the ❸ **Counting Instructions.**

IMPORTANT: If the marks don't appear within the larger boxes, check the page where you filled in the smaller boxes to see if your marks are falling high or low on the larger boxes and make the adjustment as you choose which letters to transfer.

Example:

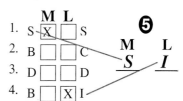

1. S ☒ S
2. B ☐ C
3. D ☐ D
4. B ☒ I

M L
S
I

	M L			M L			M L
1. S ☐☐ B	❺	33. B ☐☐ I	❺	65. D ☐☐ D	❺
2. B ☐☐ C	M L	34. B ☐☐ S	M L	66. I ☐☐ I	M L
3. D ☐☐ D	___ ___	35. D ☐☐ D	___ ___	67. S ☐☐ B	___ ___
4. I ☐☐ I		36. C ☐☐ C		68. C ☐☐ C	

5. B ☐☐ I		37. D ☐☐ D		69. B ☐☐ S	
6. D ☐☐ B	M L	38. I ☐☐ I	M L	70. B ☐☐ C	M L
7. C ☐☐ C	___ ___	39. B ☐☐ S	___ ___	71. D ☐☐ D	___ ___
8. S ☐☐ S		40. B ☐☐ C		72. I ☐☐ I	

9. B ☐☐ D		41. C ☐☐ B		73. C ☐☐ C	
10. I ☐☐ B	M L	42. S ☐☐ S	M L	74. S ☐☐ S	M L
11. S ☐☐ S	___ ___	43. I ☐☐ B	___ ___	75. D ☐☐ D	___ ___
12. C ☐☐ C		44. B ☐☐ D		76. I ☐☐ I	

13. C ☐☐ B		45. B ☐☐ I		77. B ☐☐ S	
14. B ☐☐ I	M L	46. S ☐☐ S	M L	78. I ☐☐ B	M L
15. S ☐☐ S	___ ___	47. D ☐☐ D	___ ___	79. D ☐☐ D	___ ___
16. D ☐☐ D		48. B ☐☐ B		80. C ☐☐ C	

17. D ☐☐ D	M L	49. S ☐☐ S	M L	81. I ☐☐ I	M L
18. I ☐☐ I		50. I ☐☐ I		82. B ☐☐ D	
19. C ☐☐ C	─── ───	51. D ☐☐ B	─── ───	83. S ☐☐ S	─── ───
20. S ☐☐ B		52. C ☐☐ B		84. C ☐☐ B	

21. I ☐☐ I		53. S ☐☐ S		85. D ☐☐ D	
22. C ☐☐ B	M L	54. D ☐☐ B	M L	86. I ☐☐ I	M L
23. D ☐☐ D	─── ───	55. B ☐☐ C	─── ───	87. B ☐☐ C	─── ───
24. B ☐☐ S		56. I ☐☐ I		88. S ☐☐ S	

25. S ☐☐ B		57. D ☐☐ D		89. D ☐☐ D	
26. D ☐☐ D	M L	58. S ☐☐ S	M L	90. B ☐☐ B	M L
27. I ☐☐ I	─── ───	59. C ☐☐ C	─── ───	91. C ☐☐ C	─── ───
28. C ☐☐ C		60. I ☐☐ B		92. I ☐☐ I	

29. S ☐☐ S		61. I ☐☐ B		93. B ☐☐ C	
30. B ☐☐ C	M L	62. D ☐☐ D	M L	94. I ☐☐ I	M L
31. D ☐☐ D	─── ───	63. S ☐☐ S	─── ───	95. S ☐☐ S	─── ───
32. B ☐☐ I		64. C ☐☐ B		96. D ☐☐ D	

Once you have transferred all your carbon marks to the blank "M" and "L" spaces, continue at the ❸ **Counting Instructions.**

Name_____ Date_____ Phone_____

Plotting Instructions

First complete your *Uniquely You Questionnaire*. Follow the
② INSTRUCTIONS. Once you have completed your *Uniquely You
Questionnaire* and plotted your profile, you can then continue on this page.

Once you have counted the total number of
Ds, Is, Ss, and Cs and recorded them in the
⑥ TOTAL BOXES, use those specific numbers
to plot **⑦ Graphs 1 and 2** on this page.

"M" numbers should be plotted on the
"**M**" (Graph 1) and "**L**" numbers should be
plotted on the "**L**" (Graph 2).

EXAMPLE: **TOTAL BOXES**

	D	I	S	C
	0	3	10	6

Record results from **TOTAL BOXES.**

	D	I	S	C		D	I	S	C
M":	___	___	___	___	"L":	___	___	___	___

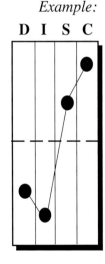

"M" Graph 1 ❼ "L" Graph 2

"M" Graph 1 — "This is expected of me"

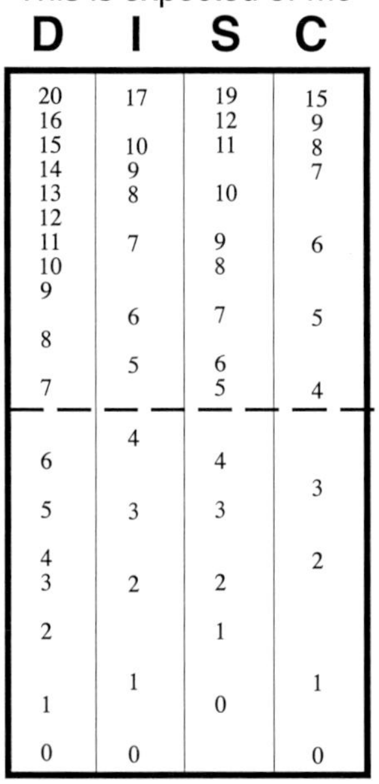

"L" Graph 2 — "This is me"

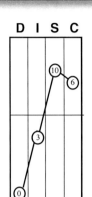

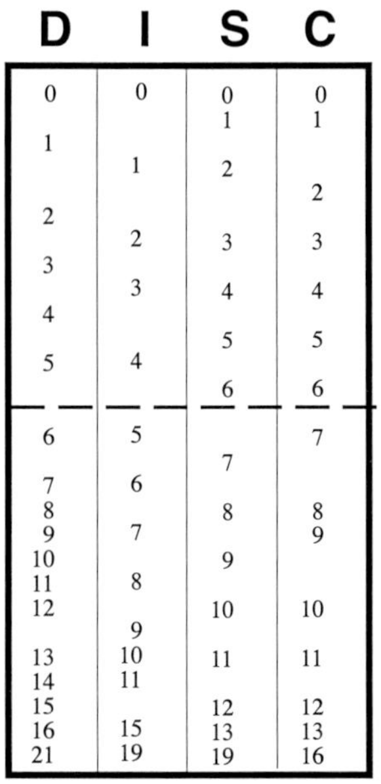

D	I	S	C
20	17	19	15
16		12	9
15	10	11	8
14	9		7
13	8	10	
12			
11	7	9	6
10		8	
9			
	6	7	5
8			
	5	6	
7		5	4
6	4	4	
			3
5	3	3	
4			2
3	2	2	
2		1	
	1		1
1		0	
0	0		0

D	I	S	C
0	0	0	0
		1	1
1			
	1	2	
			2
2	2	3	3
3			
	3	4	4
4			5
		5	
5	4		6
		6	
6	5	7	7
7	6		
8		8	8
9	7		9
10		9	
11	8		
12		10	10
	9		
13	10	11	11
14	11		
15		12	12
16	15	13	13
21	19	19	16

Note: Once you have plotted your graphs, stop thinking of them in terms of *Most* and *Least*. Graph 1 is **NOT** the *Most* you and Graph 2 is **NOT** the *Least* you. The "B"s in your Total Boxes are "blanks" and are not plotted, because they are only "norm factors." They are designed for validating your profile.

How To Read Your Graphs

1. Read the section of D, I, S or C behavior on the *Interpretation* page which corresponds with your highest plotting point on Graphs 1 and 2. Focus on the plotting point position on the graph, not the number size.

2. Personalize this information by:
• Understanding the phrases which accurately describe you.
• Ignoring phrases which don't apply.

3. Read the other sections to appreciate the general differences in the D, I, S, and C tendencies.

Look at each graph and find your highest plotting point. Notice in this example, the highest point is "C." The next highest point is "S." This profile is a "C/S" type personality.

Example:

D	I	S	C

"C/S" people are cautious and steady. They like to do one thing at a time and do it right the first time. They also like stable and secure-oriented surroundings. They don't like to take risks or cause trouble.

"C/S"s need to be more outgoing and positive. Their **Behavioral Blend** is "*Competent / Specialist.*" See *Discovering Your Behavioral Blend* to identify your specific composite behavioral type.

Remember, there is no bad personality. We need to accept the way we and others naturally respond as unique traits. Everyone doesn't think, feel or act the same way. Once we understand these differences we will be more comfortable and effective with ourselves and others.

As you read your graphs, notice your lowest plotting points. The example shows "I" as the lowest point. It means that this person doesn't enjoy inspiring or interacting with large groups of people. He or she tends to be more shy and calculating about things. This person is more reserved than outgoing. He or she likes people on an individual basis. The low "I" is not bad. It only indicates a low interest in enthusiastic and carefree behavior.

Understanding The Two Graphs

GRAPH 1: *"This is expected of me"* is your response to how you think people expect you to behave. It's your normal guarded and masked behavior.

GRAPH 2: *"This is me"* is your response to how you feel and think under pressure—how you really feel and think inside. It's your normal unguarded and unmasked behavior.

Look for the differences in Graphs 1 and 2. The higher the plotting point, the greater the intensity of that specific type of behavior. The lower the plotting point, the less the intensity of that specific type of behavior. Focus on the position high or low, rather than the number.

If Graphs 1 and 2 are alike, understanding your personality will be easier. If the two graphs are different, you may be struggling with your attitude about what is expected of you and how you want to behave. Having two different graphs is not a problem and is normal for many people.

To understand how to read the graphs at the top of this page, focus on each plotting point under the **DISC** columns. Every point above the midline is considered *high*. Every point below the mid-line is considered *low*. The higher the plotting point, the more that **DISC** letter describes your behavior. Ignore the number size.

Refer to the *Interpretation* page for what each graph specifically means in respect to the **DISC** Model of Human Behavior. Then study this entire booklet to learn "what makes you tick!"

Interpretation . . .

Be sure to first complete the ❶ *Uniquely You Questionnaire*. Follow the instructions at the top of the page. Remember to choose a focus (home or work) as you respond.

You have a predictable pattern of behavior because you have a specific personality. There are four basic personality types. These types, also known as temperaments, blend together to determine your unique personality. To help you understand why you often feel, think, and act the way you do, the following graphic summarizes the Four Temperament Model of Human Behavior.

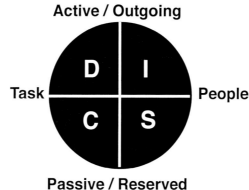

Active / Task-oriented

"D" — Dominating, directing, driving, demanding, determined, decisive, doing.

Active / Outgoing

Active / People-oriented

"I" — Inspiring, influencing, inducing, impressing, interactive, interested in people.

Task   **People**

Passive / Task-oriented

"C" — Cautious, competent, calculating, compliant, careful, contemplative.

Passive / Reserved

Passive / People-oriented

"S" — Steady, stable, shy, security-oriented, servant, submissive, specialist.

"D" BEHAVIOR / Biblical Examples: Paul & Sarah
(Active / Task-oriented) Known as "Choleric"
Descriptions: *Dominant, Direct, Demanding, Decisive*
Basic Motivation: Challenge and Control
Desires: • Freedom from control • Authority • Varied activities • Difficult assignments • Opportunities for advancement • Choices, rather than ultimatums
Responds Best To Leader Who: • Provides direct answers • Sticks to task • Gets to the point • Provides pressure • Allows freedom for personal accomplishments
Needs To Learn: • You need people • Relaxation is not a crime • Some controls are needed • Everyone has a boss • Self-control is most important • To focus on finishing well is important • Sensitivity to people's feelings is wise
Biblical Advice: BE GENTLE / NOT BOSSY — *Wisdom from above is . . . gentle,* James 3:17 • CONTROL YOUR FEELINGS AND ACTIONS — *Be angry and sin not,* Ephesians 4:26 • FOCUS ON ONE THING AT A TIME — *This ONE thing I do,* Philippians 3:13 • HAVE A SERVANT'S ATTITUDE — *By love, serve one another,* Galatians 5:13.

"I" BEHAVIOR / Biblical Examples: Peter & Ruth
(Active / People-oriented) Known as "Sanguine"
Descriptions: *Inspiring, Influencing, Impressing, Inducing*
Basic Motivation: Recognition and Approval
Desires: • Prestige • Friendly relationships • Freedom from details • Opportunities to help others • Opportunities to motivate others • Chance to verbalize ideas
Responds Best To Leader Who: • Is fair and also a friend • Provides social involvement • Provides recognition of abilities • Offers rewards for risk-taking
Needs To Learn: • Time must be managed • Deadlines are important • Too much optimism can be dangerous • Being responsible is more important than being popular • Listening better will improve one's influence.
Biblical Advice: BE HUMBLE / AVOID PRIDE — *Humble yourself in the SIGHT of God,* James 3:17 • CONTROL YOUR SPEECH — *Be quick to hear, slow to speak,* James 1:19 • BE MORE ORGANIZED — *Do all things decently and in order,* 1 Corinthians 14:40 • BE PATIENT — *The fruit of the Spirit is . . . longsuffering,* Galatians 5:23.

"C" BEHAVIOR / Biblical Examples: Thomas & Esther
(Passive / Task-oriented) Known as "Melancholy"
Descriptions: *Competent, Compliant, Cautious, Calculating*
Basic Motivation: Quality and Correctness
Desires: • Clearly defined tasks • Details • Limited risks • Assignments that require precision and planning • Time to think
Responds Best To Leader Who: • Provides reassurance • Spells out detailed operating procedures • Provides resources to do task correctly • Listens to suggestions
Needs To Learn: • Total support is not always possible • Thorough explanation is not everything • Deadlines must be met • More optimism will lead to greater success
Biblical Advice: BE MORE POSITIVE — *Whatsoever things are lovely, of good report ... think on these things,* Philippians 4:8 • AVOID A BITTER AND CRITICAL SPIRIT — *Let all bitterness . . be put away from you,* Ephesians 4:31 • BE JOYFUL — *The fruit of the Spirit is . . . joy,* Galatians 5:22 • DON'T WORRY — *Fret not,* Psalm 37:1.

"S" BEHAVIOR / Biblical Examples: Moses & Hannah
(Passive / People-oriented) Known as "Phlegmatic"
Descriptions: *Submissive, Steady, Stable, Security-oriented*
Basic Motivation: Stability and Support
Desires: • An area of specialization • Identification with a group • Established work patterns • Security of situation • Consistent familiar environment
Responds Best To Leader Who: • Is relaxed and friendly • Allows time to adjust to changes • Allows to work at own pace • Gives personal support
Needs To Learn: • Change provides opportunity • Friendship isn't everything • Discipline is good • Boldness and taking risks is sometimes necessary
Biblical Advice: BE BOLD AND STRONG — *Only be strong and very courageous,* Joshua 1:6 • BE CONFIDENT AND FEARLESS — *God has not given you the spirit of fear,* 2 Timothy 1:7 • BE MORE ENTHUSIASTIC — *Whatsoever you do, do it HEARTILY as unto the Lord,* Colossians 3:23.

DISCOVERING YOUR BEHAVIORAL BLEND

There are four basic personality types known as **D, I, S,** and **C** behavior. Everyone is a blend or combination of these four temperaments. No type is better than the other. No one has a bad personality. The most important factor is what you do with your personality. Don't let your personality control you; instead learn how to control your personality.

To help you discover more about your specific behavioral style, there are 21 **Behavioral Blends.** One or two **Behavioral Blends** will best describe you. Few people are pure **D, I, S,** or **C** types. Most everyone is a combination of the four types. Remember, it doesn't matter what personality you have, as much as what you do with it.   (Continue instructions next page.)

D: DETERMINED DOERS

"D"s are dominant and demanding. They win at all costs. They do not care as much about what people think as they care about getting the job done. Their insensitivity to feelings makes them too strong. They are great at developing things, but they need to improve their ability to do things correctly. Their strong will should be disciplined to prepare and think more accurately about what they are doing. They are motivated by serious challenges to accomplish tasks.

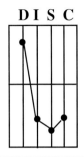

D/I: DRIVING INFLUENCERS

"D/I"s are bottom line people. They are much like Dynamic Influencers. They are a little more determined and less inspirational, but they are strong doers and able to induce others to follow. They need to be more cautious and careful, as well as more steady and stable. They get involved in a lot of projects at the same time. They need to focus on one thing at a time and slow down. They are motivated by opportunities to accomplish great tasks through a lot of people.

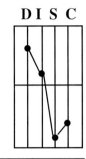

I: INSPIRATIONAL INFLUENCERS

"I"s are impressive people. They are extremely active and excited individuals. Approval is important to them. They can have lots of friends if they do not overdo their need for attention. They can be sensitive and emotional. They need to be more interested in others and willing to listen. They do not like research unless it makes them look good. They often do things to please the crowd. They are entertainers. They need to control their feelings and think more logically. They often outshine others and are motivated by recognition.

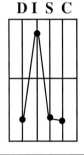

I/D: INSPIRATIONAL DOERS

"I/D"s are super salespeople. They love large groups. They are impressive and can easily influence people to do things. They need a lot of recognition. They exaggerate and often talk too much. They jump into things without thinking them through. They need to be more studious and still. They should also be more careful and cautious. They are motivated by exciting opportunities to do difficult things. If not careful, they will do things to please the crowd and get themselves into trouble in the process. They make inspiring leaders and determined individuals.

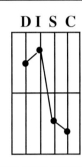

S: STEADY SPECIALISTS

"S"s are stable and shy types. They do not like changes. They enjoy pleasing people and can consistently do the same job. Secure, non-threatening surroundings are important to them. They make the best friends because they are so forgiving. Other people sometimes take advantage of them. They need to be stronger and learn how to say, "No" to a friend who wants them to do wrong. Talking in front of large crowds is difficult for them. They are motivated by sweet and sincere opportunities to help others.

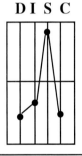

S/I: STEADY INFLUENCERS

"S/I"s are sensitive and inspirational. They accept and represent others well. They have lots of friends because they are tolerant and forgiving. They do not hurt people's feelings and can be very influential. They need to be more task-oriented. They must learn to finish their work and do it well. They like to talk, but should pay more attention to instructions. They would be more influential if they were more aggressive and careful. They are kind and considerate. Motivated by opportunities to share and shine, they induce others to follow.

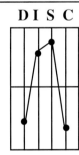

C: CAUTIOUS COMPETENT TYPES

"C"s are logical and analytical. Their predominant drive is careful, calculating, compliant and correct behavior. When frustrated, they can over do it or be the exact opposite. They need answers and opportunities to reach their potential. They tend not to care about the feelings of others. They can be critical and picky. They prefer quality and reject phoniness in others. They are motivated by explanations and projects that stimulate their thinking.

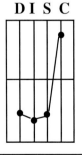

C/S: COMPETENT SPECIALISTS

"C/S"s tend to always be right. They like to do one thing at a time and do it right the first time. Their steady and stable approach to things makes them sensitive. They tend to be reserved and cautious. They are consistent and careful, but seldom take risks or try new things. They do not like speaking to large crowds, but will work hard behind the scenes to help groups stay on track. They are motivated by opportunities to serve others and to do things correctly.

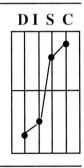

I/D/S: INSPIRING DRIVING SUBMISSIVE

"I/D/S"s are impressing, demanding and stabilizing at the same time. They are not as cautious and calculating as those with more "C" tendencies. They are more active than passive. But they also have sensitivity and steadiness. They may seem to be more people-oriented, but can be dominant and decisive in their task-orientation. They need to be more contemplative and conservative. Details don't seem as important as taking charge and working with people.

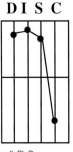

D/I/C: DOMINANT INSPIRING CAUTIOUS

"D/I/C"s are demanding, impressing and competent. They tend to be more task-oriented, but can be people-oriented before crowds. They need to increase their sensitivity and softness. They don't mind change. Active and outgoing, they are also compliant and cautious. They like to do things correctly, while driving and influencing others to follow. Their verbal skills combine with their determination and competence to achieve. Security is not as important as accomplishment and looking good.

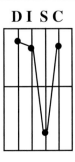

Observe the 21 **Behavioral Blends** on these two pages. Choose the one or two profiles that are most like your graphs. Read the brief paragraph descriptions of the ones that are most like you. You will probably be a combination of two specific profiles. You can also have some characteristics of other types, but will normally fit into one or two **Behavioral Blends**.

Every personality has strengths and weaknesses (uniquenesses). One person's weakness may be another person's strength. That's why "uniqueness" may be a better word than "weakness." In order to be more successful and improve your relationships, you must learn how to control your strengths and avoid your "uniquenesses." Always remember that under pressure you lean toward your strengths. The over-use of a strength becomes an abuse, and the best thing about you becomes the worst. The characteristic that people once liked most about you can become what they later despise.

D/I: DYNAMIC INFLUENCERS

D I S C

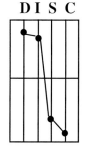

"D/I"s are impressive, demanding types. They get excited about accomplishing tasks and looking good. Determined and driven, they influence large crowds best. They can be too strong and concerned about what others think. They have good communication skills and are interested in people. They need to be more sensitive and patient with the feelings of others. Learning to slow down and think through projects are crucial for them. They are motivated by opportunities to control and impress.

D/C: DRIVING COMPETENT TYPES

D I S C

"D/C" Types are determined students or defiant critics. They want to be in charge, while collecting information to accomplish tasks. They care more about getting a job done and doing it right than what others think or feel. They drive themselves and others. They are dominant and caustic. Improving their people skills is important. They need to be more sensitive and understanding. They are motivated by choices and challenges to do well.

I/S: INSPIRATIONAL SPECIALISTS

D I S C

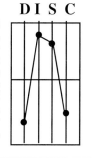

"I/S"s are influential and stable. They love people and people love them. They like to please and serve others. They do not like time controls or difficult tasks. They want to look good and encourage others, but often lack organizational skills. They follow directions and do what they are told. They should be more concerned about what to do, than with whom to do it. They are motivated by interactive and sincere opportunities to help others. Regardless of being up front or behind the scenes, they influence and support others. They make great friends, colleagues, and obedient workers.

I/C: INSPIRATIONAL COMPETENT

D I S C

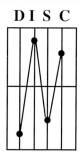

"I/C" Types are inspiring, yet cautious. They size up situations and comply with the rules in order to look good. They are good at figuring out ways to do things better through a lot of people. They can be too persuasive and too concerned about winning. They are often impatient and critical. They need to be more sensitive to individual feelings. They are often more concerned about what others think. They do not like breaking the rules; neither do they enjoy taking risks. They need to try new things and sometimes go against the crowd. They are careful communicators who think things through.

S/D: STEADY DOERS

D I S C

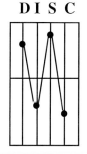

S/D"s get the job done. They prefer stable surroundings and are determined to accomplish tasks. As quiet leaders, they relate best to small groups. They do not like to talk in front of large crowds, but want to control them. They enjoy secure relationships, but often dominate them. They can be soft and hard at the same time. They are motivated by sincere challenges that allow them to systematically do great things. They prefer sure things, rather than shallow recognition. They make good colleagues, while driving to succeed.

S/C: STEADY COMPETENT TYPES

D I S C

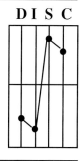

"S/C" Types are stable and contemplative types. They like to search and discover the facts. They like to weigh the evidence and proceed slowly to a logical conclusion. They enjoy small groups of people. They do not like speaking in front of large crowds. They are systematic and sensitive to the needs of others, but can be critical and caustic. They are loyal friends, but can be too fault-finding. They need to improve their enthusiasm and optimism. They are motivated by kind and conscientious opportunities to slowly and correctly do things.

C/I/S: COMPETENT INFLUENCING SPECIALISTS

D I S C

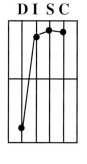

"C/I/S"s like to do things right, impress others and stabilize situations. They are not aggressive or pushy people. They enjoy large and small crowds. They are good with people and prefer quality. They are sensitive to what others think about them and their work. They need to be more determined and dominant. They can do things well, but are poor at quick decision-making. They are capable of doing great things through people, but need to be more self-motivated and assertive. They are stimulated by sincere, enthusiastic approval and logical explanations.

C/S/D: COMPETENT STEADY DOERS

D I S C

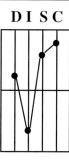

"C/S/D"s are a combination of cautious, stable and determined types. They are more task-oriented, but care about people on an individual basis. They don't like to speak in front of crowds. They prefer to get the job done and do it right through small groups, as opposed to large groups. They tend to be more serious. Often misunderstood by others as being insensitive, "C/S/D" types really care for people. They just don't show it openly. They need to be more positive and enthusiastic. Natural achievers, they need to be more friendly and less critical.

STRAIGHT MID-LINE

D I S C

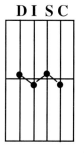

A Straight Mid-Line Blend occurs when all four plotting points are close together in the middle of the graph. This may indicate that the person is trying to please everyone. Striving to be "all things to all men" may indicate mature response to pressure. Or it may confirm frustration over the intensity differences under pressure. The person may be saying, "I really don't know what my D, I, S, or C behavior should be or really is." The person may want to do another profile after a while to see if there is any change.

ABOVE MID-LINE • BELOW MID-LINE

D I S C

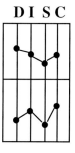

Some patterns indicate unique struggles an individual may be having.

An Above Mid-Line Blend occurs when all four plotting points are above the mid-line. This may indicate a strong desire to overachieve.

A Below Mid-Line Blend occurs when all four plotting points are below the mid-line. This may indicate that the person is not really sure how to respond to challenges.

15

CONTROLLING YOUR BEHAVIORAL BLEND

The "bottom line" is allowing the Holy Spirit to control your personality. People often say, "*I just want to be me.*" They want to find themselves and be "real." The problem is when you really find yourself, you often don't like what you find. You might be so dictatorial, self-seeking, insecure or critical that God seems powerless in your life. The so-called "real" or natural you can be opposite of what God wants you to be. You should not seek to be normal, but spiritual; not natural, but supernatural — to do what you do through the power of God in your life, to be what God wants you to be through a personal relationship with Him by faith in Jesus Christ as your Savior and Lord (Ephesians 2:8-10). **Be conformed into the image of Christ.** (Continue instructions next page.)

D: DETERMINED DOERS

Be careful to not offend when you take charge—"The servant of the Lord must not strive (be pushy), but be gentle," 2 Timothy 2:24. Anger is normal, but must be controlled—"Be angry and sin not," Ephesians 4:26. Be motivated to purity and peace—"Wisdom from above is first pure, peaceable . . .," James 3:17. Focus on doing ONE thing well—"This ONE thing I do," Philippians 3:13. Always remember, God is the Master of your fate—"The fear of the Lord is the beginning of wisdom," Proverbs 1:7.

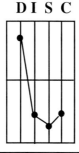

D/I: DRIVING INFLUENCERS

Though naturally fearless and able, you need to respect God's power over you—"Fear God and give Him glory," Revelations 14:7. Guard the over-use of strength and be kind — "By the meekness and gentleness of Christ," 2 Corinthians 10:1. Making peace is a greater challenge than winning a fight—"Blessed are the peacemakers," Matthew 5:9. Choose words carefully—"A soft answer turns away wrath," Proverbs 15:1. God must control your feelings—"The fruit of the Spirit is . . . temperance (self-control)," Galatians 5:23.

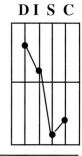

I: INSPIRATIONAL INFLUENCERS

Don't exalt yourself—"Humble yourself and God will exalt you," James 4:10. Be sure to listen more—"quick to hear, slow to speak," James 1:19. Work at being organized—"Do all things decently and in order," 1 Corinthians 14:40. Concentrate on doing what is most important—"All things are not expedient," 1 Corinthians 10:23. Prepare more—"Prepare yourself," 2 Chron. 35:4. Be careful what you desire—"Delight in the Lord," Psalm 37:4. Don't be over-confident and watch what you promise—Peter claimed he would never deny Christ, Mark 14:31.

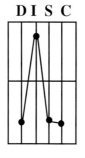

I/D: INSPIRATIONAL DOERS

Guard the power of your words—"The tongue is a fire," James 3:6. Don't be like those who "by fair words and good speeches—deceive," Romans 16:18. Always tell the truth—"Speak the truth and lie not," 1 Timothy 2:7. Remember Who has blessed you—"God must increase, I must decrease," John 3:30. Give God the glory for all you do—"Give unto the Lord glory," Psalm 29:1,2. Put God first in your life—"Seek you first the kingdom of God," Matthew 6:33. Beware of—The "lust of the flesh and pride of life;" they will ultimately destroy your talents, 1 John 2:16.

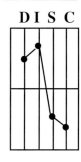

S: STEADY SPECIALISTS

Increase your confidence in Christ—"I can do all things through Christ, Who strengthens me," Philippians 4:13. God is your—"rock, fortress and deliverer," Psalm 18:2. Fearfulness is not from God—"God has not given you the spirit of fear," 2 Timothy 1:7. Speak out more—"Let the redeemed of the Lord say so," Psalm 107:2. Be more outgoing and less inhibited—"Christ has made us free," Galatians 5:1. Be more assertive—Moses confronted Pharaoh with "let my people go," Ex. 5:1. Security is possible—"You are secure, because of hope," Job 11:18.

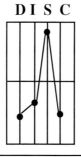

S/I: STEADY INFLUENCERS

Speak out—"Bold to speak without fear," Philippians 1:14. Take stands—"Stand fast in one spirit," Philippians 4:1. The Spirit of God can help you tell others about Christ—"The Spirit of the Lord is upon me," Isaiah 61:1. Guard against fearfulness—"Let not your heart be troubled, neither let it be afraid," Luke 14:27. Remember, you don't need "people" to encourage you—"David encouraged himself in the Lord," 1 Samuel 30:6. Always do right and don't fear people—"Fear of man brings a snare (trap)," Psalm 29:25.

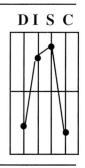

C: CAUTIOUS COMPETENT TYPES

Be more patient when wanting to correct others—"Rebuke, exhort with all longsuffering," 2 Timothy 4:2. Correct in love—"Speak the truth in love," Ephesians 4:15. Be more positive—"Rejoice in the Lord ALWAYS," Philippians 4:4. Hope in God, not circumstances—"Rejoicing in hope," Romans 12:12. The most logical thing you can do is serve God—"Present your bodies a living sacrifice . . . which is your reasonable service," Rom 12:2. Find happiness in God—"Delight in the Lord," Psalm 37:4.

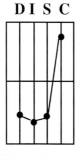

C/S: COMPETENT SPECIALISTS

Think more positively—"Whatsoever things are pure . . . of good report . . . think on those things," Philippians 4:8,9. Guard against the fear of failure—God promises "Fear not for I am with you," Isaiah 43:5. Focus on the possible—"With God all things are possible," Matthew 19:26. Be cheerful—"The fruit of the Spirit is . . . joy," Galatians 5:22. When everything goes wrong, God is all you need—"Our sufficiency is of God," 2 Corinthians 3:5. Think like Christ—"Let this mind be in you which was also in Christ," Philippians 4:8.

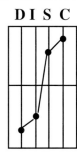

I/D/S: INSPIRING DRIVING SUBMITTING

Be more calculating and careful—"Sit down first and count the cost," Luke 14:28. Organize yourself and attempt to be more organized, "Do all things decently and in order," 1 Corinthians 14:40. Be careful what you promise—"Let your 'yea' be 'yea' and your 'nay' be 'nay'," 2 Corinthians 1:17. Give God the glory for all you do—"Give unto the Lord glory," Psalm 29:1,2. Think before you do things — "A wise man thinks to know," Ecc. 8:17. Be humble and share the glory — "Humble yourself and God will exalt you," James 4:10.

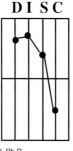

D/I/C: DOMINANT INSPIRING CAUTIOUS

Be sure to listen more—"quick to hear, slow to speak," James 1:19. Be more sensitive to the individual's feelings — "The servant of the Lord must not strive, but be gentle," 2 Timothy 2:24. Be more of a peacemaker—"Blessed are the peacemakers," Matthew 5:9. Be more steady and don't get sidetracked—"Be steadfast always doing the work of the Lord," 1 Corinthians 15:58. Don't be judgmental — "If a man be overtaken in a fault, restore him," Galatians 6:1.

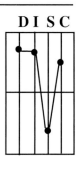

Once you discover your **Behavioral Blend/s**, you can clearly recognize the areas God wants to work on. The Bible is the best source to help you. *"All Scripture is given by inspiration of God and is profitable for doctrine, for reproof, for correction, for instruction in righteousness"* (2 Timothy 3:16). The following are specific scriptures each **Behavioral Blend** should consider. These scriptures are admonitions and challenges to help you focus on becoming more like Christ. You should grow spiritually to the place in your life where people really don't know what personality you have. Balance and maturity should be your goal. Ask God to use these scriptures to encourage and empower you. Don't let them discourage you. The Word of God is quick and powerful, sharper than any two-edged sword. It can discern and deliver you from a self-centered attitude of "me-ism." Learn to be so controlled by the Holy Spirit that God gets the glory in all you say and do (Ephesians 5:18).

D/I: DYNAMIC INFLUENCERS

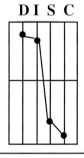

Concentrate on humility and obedience—Christ "humbled Himself and became obedient," Philippians 2:8. Everyone has a boss, even you—the centurion said to Jesus, "I too am a man under authority," Matthew 8:9. Avoid rebellion —"Rebellion is as the sin of witchcraft," 1 Samuel 15:23. Winning is not always most important—"The first shall be last," Matthew 19:30. Be patient with others—"The fruit of the Spirit is longsuffering," Galatians 5:23. Learn to relax in the Lord, not in your ability to make things happen—"Rest in the Lord," Psalm 37:7.

D/C: DRIVING COMPETENT TYPES

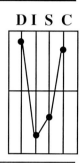

Seek to get along with everyone—"Live peaceably with all men," Romans 12:18. Be kind and loving—"Kindly affectionate one to another," Romans 12:10. Show more love—"Love one another," 1 John 4:7. Seek to serve, not to be served—Be a "servant of Christ," Ephesians 6:6. Meekness is not weakness. Control your desire to have power over others. Be Christlike—"By the meekness and gentleness of Christ," 2 Corinthians 10:1. Take time to be still and commune with God—"Be still and know that I am God," Psalm 46:10.

I/S: INSPIRATIONAL SPECIALISTS

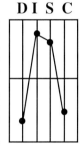

Do everything unto the Lord—"Whatsoever you do, do it heartily, as unto the Lord and not unto men," Colossians 3:23. Beware of seeking man's approval—"Not with eye-service as men pleasers," Ephesians 6:6. Seek to please God, rather than others—"Do always those things that please Him," John 8:29. Be more task-oriented—"Sit down first and count the cost," Luke 14:28. Don't be lazy—"not slothful in business," Romans 12:11. Work hard—"Let every man prove his work," Galatians 6:4. Don't just talk about what you want—"Being fruitful in every good work," Colossians 1:10. Be industrious—"Night comes when no one will work," John 9:4.

I/C: INSPIRATIONAL COMPETENT

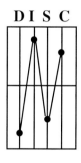

Be careful you don't think too highly of yourself—"God resists the proud, but gives grace to the humble," 1 Peter 5:5. Seek to please God more than others—"When a man's ways please the Lord," Proverbs 16:7. Be a good example—"Be an example of the believer," 1 Timothy 4:12. Care more about how you look to God—"Glorify God in your body and spirit," 1 Corinthians 6:20. Be bold and confident in Christ—"We have boldness and access with confidence by the faith of Him," Ephesians 3:12. Guard statements and judgments —"A lying tongue is a vanity tossed to and fro," Proverbs 21:6. Don't flatter yourself—"He flatters himself in his own eyes," Psalm 36:2.

S/D: STEADY DOERS

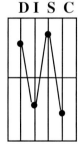

God wants to empower what you think is weakness—"Most gladly will I rather glory in my infirmities that the power of Christ may rest upon me." God's grace (the power and ability to do what God wants) is enough for whatever you need—"My grace is sufficient for you." You are often strongest in weakness, as you trust in God and not yourself—"For when I am weak, then am I strong," 2 Corinthians 12:9. Encourage and help others daily—"Exhort one another daily," Hebrews 3:13. God challenges you to reason with Him—"Come now and let us reason together," Isaiah 1:18.

S/C: STEADY COMPETENT TYPES

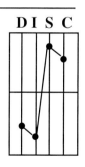

Be assertive and stronger—"Only be strong and very courageous," Joshua 1:6. Be more enthusiastic—"Whatever you do, do it heartily," Colossians 3:23. Enjoy relationships, rather than endure them—Christ said, "I am come that you might have life . . . abundantly," John 10:10. Peace and happiness do not come from security and safety —"Peace I leave with you, my peace I give unto you," John 14:27. Divine peace is knowing God's ways are beyond ours—"The peace of God passes all understanding," Philippians 4:7. Be fearless in Christ—"I will fear no evil," Psalm 23:4.

C/I/S: COMPETENT INFLUENCING SPECIALISTS

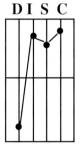

Guard against being judgmental—"Judge not lest you be judged," Matthew 7:1. "Who are you that judges another," James 4:12. Avoid bitterness and resentment—"Lest any root of bitterness spring up to trouble you," Hebrews 12:15. God will meet your needs—"My God shall supply all your need according to His riches in glory," Philippians 4:19. Be thankful for everything—"In all things give thanks," 1 Thess. 5:18. Let God's Word affect you—"Let the Word of God dwell in you richly in all wisdom," Colossians 3:16. Whatever you do, do it for God's glory—"Do all in the name of God," Colossians 3:17.

C/S/D: COMPETENT STEADY DOERS

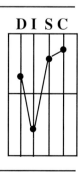

Be more enthusiastic—"Whatever you do, do it heartily as unto the Lord," Colossians 3:23. Don't worry so much about problems — "Let not your heart be troubled," John 14:27. Be more positive — "Whatsoever things are pure . . . if there be any virtue, think on these things," Philippians 4:8,9. Let your sensitivity be more evident — "Be kindly affectionate, one to another," Romans 12:10. Don't be like Moses when he was reluctant to lead because of his poor verbal skills (Exodus 4:10-16). Be more outwardly optimistic and encouraging to others — "Exhort one another daily," Hebrews 3:13.

STRAIGHT MID-LINE

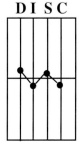

You may be trying to be all things to all men, which is good, but can be frustrating at times. The farther apart your plotting points, the easier it is to read the profile. Recognize your identity in Christ — "I am crucified with Christ, nevertheless I live, yet not I, but Christ lives in me," Galatians 2:20. Relax in the Lord — "Come unto me all you that labor and are heavy laden and I will give you rest," Matthew 11:28. You cannot please everyone all the time — "Having men's persons in admiration," Jude 16.

ABOVE MID-LINE • BELOW MID-LINE

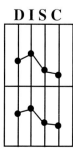

An Above Mid-Line Blend may be trying to over-achieve — "It is God who works in us, both to will and do of His good pleasure," Philippians 2:13. You may be thinking too highly of what is expected of you or the real you. Remember Peter.

A Below Mid-Line Blend may indicate you are not really sure how to respond to challenges — "I can do all things through Christ," Philippians 4:13. Think more positively about yourself — "I am fearfully and wonderfully made," Psalm 139:14.

17

COMBINING PERSONALITIES WITH SPIRITUAL GIFTS

The following are combinations of D, I, S, and C type personalities with sixteen Spiritual Gifts. Be sure to also read the instructions at the top of the next page.

First, identify which letter (D, I, S or C) best describes your personality type. This can be done by finding the highest plotting point/s on Graphs 1 & 2.

Then notice your most obvious Spiritual Gift/s. Do this by finding the highest plotting point/s in your Spiritual Gifts Profile graph.

There are 64 combinations of 4 personality types and 16 Spiritual Gifts. Find the description/s of your combinations. You may have several combinations to identify.

Consider the insights that most describe you and disregard those that are not like you. Keep in mind, you are a blend of behaviors and gifts. Prayerfully study each description, asking God to control your personality and Spiritual Gift/s for His glory.

Study this booklet to also find where God can use you in ministry. Discovering your personality and Spiritual Gift/s should result in maturity and involvement in the Body of Christ. Grow for it!

"D" Type Personalities With Administration / Ruling

Demanding type Christians with the Gift of Administration are strong leaders. They like to tell others what to do. They often see what needs to be done and delegate the work to others. They can be too bossy. "D"-Administrators tend to see the big picture, but lack warmth to get others to help without pressure. They can intimidate and offend if not careful. Often concerned more about tasks, than people, they need to be sensitive and loving. "D"-Administrators can be gifted leaders who press forward to do great things for God.

"I" Type Personalities With Administration / Ruling

Influencing type Christians with the Gift of Administration are optimistic leaders. Their positive enthusiasm encourages others to get involved. They can be overly excited. They tend to talk people into doing things they don't want to do. They impress others with their friendliness and verbal skills. "I"-Administrators need to guard against manipulating. They should serve by example. They often take on more than they can handle, disappointing those who expect a lot from them. However, they can accomplish much through people.

"D" Type Personalities With The Gift of Apostleship

Christians who are driven to start new churches often have the Gift of Apostleship. They like impossible challenges. "D" type Apostles / Pioneering today are determined and demanding. They don't let obstacles get in their way. They plod through the thick and thin of birthing something from nothing. They are determined to organize new ministries, especially among different cultural and ethnic groups. They are active, task-oriented individuals who demonstrate tremendous confidence and authority.

"I" Type Personalities With The Gift of Apostleship

Christians who constantly use their influence and enthusiasm to start new churches often have the Gift of Apostleship / Pioneering. They tend to be inspiring and energetic about reaching other groups, especially those of other cultures. Those with "I" type personalities and the Gift of Apostleship are active, people-oriented individuals. They tend to step out into unchartered regions in order to start new ministries. They make great impressions while using their authority, but should guard their excitement.

"D" Type Personalities With the Gift of Discernment

Active / task-oriented Christians with unusual discernment about right and wrong are "D" type personalities with the Gift of Discernment. They tend to be pushy and controlling with their discernment. They have great insights, but often use it in a demanding and driving way. They enjoy using their discernment to confront or challenge others to obey God's Word. They need to be more sensitive and compassionate concerning what they feel is about a particular problem.

"I" Type Personalities With The Gift of Discernment

Christians who constantly inspire and influence others through their discernment of right and wrong are often "I" type personalities with the Gift of Discernment. They seem to flaunt their discernment and are sometimes come across as boastful. Those who use their intuitive senses to encourage and lift-up others often have active / people-oriented personalities. They make great impacts on people. They are enthusiastic and get real excited when they can use what they discern about things to help others.

"D" Type Personalities With The Gift of Evangelism

Dynamic and demanding type Christians with the Gift of Evangelism can be extremely effective. They are self-starters with a sense of urgency. But their driving concern to win souls can make them too pushy. "D"-Evangelists should be more gentle and patient. Determined to get the job done, they often feel like everyone should be involved in evangelism. Direct with their presentations, they like sermons that explain the gospel and offer invitations to trust Christ. "D"- Evangelists are dedicated to *"making Him known."*

"I" Type Personalities With The Gift of Evangelism

Influencing type Christians with the Gift of Evangelism are most enthusiastic about soul winning. They are also very contagious — cheerleaders for Christ. Interested in people, they are "natural-born" witnesses. "I"-Evangelists make sharing the gospel look so easy. Because of their strong desire to impress, they may care equally about what people think of them and leading others to Christ. They must constantly remember God gave them gifts to shine for Him, not self. "I"-Evangelists can win many souls to Christ.

The unique feature of these 64 combinations is to understand how your specific personality type relates to your spiritual gifts. There are dichotomies — unique blends and combinations. No one has a bad composite blend. Many combinations are more common than others, but there is no wrong or abnormal combination.

There are uncommon blends (but not abnormal blends); such as, the Gift of Showing Mercy and a "D" type personality. Most people with Showing Mercy have "S" personalities. But God sometimes gives certain people this unique combination. It's a "strange bedfellow" or "oxymoron", like "gentle strength" or a "velvet covered brick." The two don't seem to mix or mesh, but God makes no mistakes and does what He pleases to gift you for His glory.

A Christian with a "D" type personality and the Gift of Showing Mercy is the kind that will bite your head off and then apologize or ask for your forgiveness. An "S" type personality and the Gift of Prophecy is also like the person who will bite your head off and then cry about it. The Prophet Jeremiah is a good example of this dichotomy combination.

It doesn't matter what your composite blends of spiritual gifts and personality are. What really matters is, are you aware of how your different motivations affect you and do you allow the Holy Spirit to control the different influences that motivate you? Don't let your natural and supernatural motivations control you. Let God control your motivations!

Study all the combinations to see if there may be any others that describe you. Above all, remember God made you unique — to discover and exercise your giftedness for His glory.

"S" Type Personalities With Administration / Ruling

Submissive type Christians with the Gift of Administration are concerned about getting tasks done in steady and stable ways. They need to be more assertive and aggressive. "S"-Administrators can be too sacrificing. They are faithful in whatever they do, but need to inspire others to help. They can be quiet leaders, challenging others by example. They tend to be shy. Sometimes, they surprise others with their serious concern to accomplish tasks. "S"-Administrators are achievers who like to work through small groups.

"C" Type Personalities With Administration / Ruling

Cautious type Christians with the Gift of Administration are competent task-masters. They see a need and organize others to meet that need. They enjoy doing things completely right the first time. They tend to be picky. They can increase effectiveness with more warmth and team participation. Working through people and creating an enthusiastic atmosphere can he helpful. They should avoid being critical of what others do. "C"-Administrators are best able to get groups to do the right things.

"S" Type Personalities With The Gift of Apostleship

Steady and stable type Christians who are uncharacteristically passionate about starting new ministries may have the Gift of Apostleship / Pioneering. They are slow and shy, but determined about their ideas. They are consistent and don't give up easily. They don't have to always be up front, but are compassionate and sensitive about reaching out to other groups. Those with "S" type personalities with the Gift of Apostleship have a quiet, but a strong vision and authority about starting new churches.

"C" Type Personalities With The Gift of Apostleship

Typically cautious and calculating Christians who are committed to starting new churches often have the Gift of Apostleship / Pioneering. They tend to be overly careful and research things to death. But their plans and programs are just what new churches need. They don't mind standing alone. They are passive, task-oriented individuals. They are stimulated by the need for organization. They enjoy putting people and programs together to start ministries, often to different types of cultures and groups.

"S" Type Personalities With The Gift of Discernment

The more passive / people-oriented Christians with great intuition often have "S" type personalities with the Gift of Discernment. They are not pushy or controlling. They are often very quiet and wait for opportunities to share what they discern about a problem. They especially love to share how the Word of God applies to a particular situation. They are often very shy. They don't like to make others uncomfortable, but can be a tremendous friend and source of encouragement and direction.

"C" Type Personalities With The Gift of Discernment

Compliant and calculating types with unusual intuition often have "C" type personalities with the Gift of Discernment. They tend to be picky and often "too" right for most people to appreciate. But they make the greatest resource when it comes to making practical decisions. This combination is best at choosing the right direction, but needs to be more sensitive to how their discernment might affect others. With more inspiring and optimistic attitudes, this combination is so powerful and respected.

"S" Type Personalities With The Gift of Evangelism

Sweet and soft type Christians with the Gift of Evangelism are the most gentle witnesses. They steadily share the gospel. They don't like to force issues. They tend to be too nice. Scoffers often waste "S"-Evangelists' time. Knowing they will go the extra mile, some people take advantage. Avoiding confrontation, these stable types prefer "friendship evangelism." But their motivation to win souls often overcomes their natural reluctance to speak out. "S"-Evangelists enjoy bringing people to Jesus without a lot of fanfare.

"C" Type Personalities With The Gift of Evangelism

Cautious and compliant type Christians with the Gift of Evangelism are the most thorough witnesses. They like to go point-by-point, convincing people to understand every detail. They try to have an answer for every question. But they can overwhelm with too many facts. "C"-Evangelists are often more concerned with the task, rather than the person in need. As competent individuals, they need to be more flexible and friendly. "C"-Evangelists can turn doubt into a fascinating opportunity for Christ.

"D" Type Personalities With The Gift of Encouraging

Decisive type Christians with the Gift of Encouraing are persistent exhorters. They tend to dominate conversations with practical steps-of-action. They like to share advice. "D" Exhorters are driven to control the situation in order to encourage. They need to be more flexible and sensitive. People can't always do or feel what "D"-Exhorters want. They tend to have a plan for every problem. Often impatient, they can be too pushy. Letting others share their ideas, while determined to encourage others, makes them extremely effective.

"I" Type Personalities With The Gift of Encouraging

Inspiring type Christians with the Gift of Encouraging make enthusiastic exhorters. They impress others with their advice. But they can be too optimistic. They often create high expectations. They need to be more realistic. "I"-Exhorters should guard against using their verbal skills to manipulate others. They may try to influence others to do more than humanly possible. They should listen more and speak less. Interested in others, they often induce positive responses. "I"-Exhorters communicate encouragement best.

"D" Type Personalities With The Gift of Faith

Active / task-oriented Christians who constantly demonstrate an unusual amount of dependence upon God often have the Gift of Faith. They tend to be more demanding than most people. They often challenge others to have more faith. They are stimulated by the Word of God to increase their faith. They are very driven and decisive. They don't take a long time to make up their minds. They like to move forward in faith once the decision has been made. They tend to have great faith when things look hopeless.

"I" Type Personalities With The Gift of Faith

Christians who get most excited about believing God often have the Gift of Faith. They are extremely enthusiastic and inspire others to increase their faith. They are very expressive and talk a lot about the joy of trusting the Lord for everything. "I" type personalities with the Gift of Faith are sometimes too optimistic and rush in where angels fear to tread. They need to be more cautious and guard their faith from making miscalculated decisions. But they make great encouragers in difficult times.

"D" Type Personalities With The Gift of Giving

Domineering type Christians with the Gift of Giving are serious about financial matters. They can be very successful in business. They also have the "gift of getting." They tend to use money to control others. Demanding how finances are used, they can be extremely picky with budgets. They seldom give to the wheel that squeaks the loudest. They are either unbending or influencing, when it comes to financial decisions. They either discourage or encourage others with their money and / or advice. They can make great financial counselors.

"I" Type Personalities With The Gift of Giving

Impressing type Christians with the Gift of Giving are enthusiastic about stewardship. They like to encourage everyone to be givers. They make great promoters, but can kill projects because of financial concerns. "I"-Givers are more optimistic than others. They can be too positive. Their faith is evident in giving, but can become prideful. They like to tell everyone how to give more. When discouraged, they may use their verbal skills and financial credibility to influence others. "I"-Givers are most excited when it involves finances.

"D" Type Personalities With The Gift of Hospitality

Christians who are demanding, but always volunteering their homes for meetings or for those needing a place to stay often have the Gift of Hospitality. They are active / task-oriented individuals who are driven and determined to make their home a blessing to others. They tend to be controlling, but willing to be taken advantage of when it comes to hospitality. They love to plan meetings and entertain people in their homes, but are always in charge.

"I" Type Personalities With The Gift of Hospitality

Enthusiastic and excited Christians who love to invite others to their homes often have the Gift of Hospitality. The are "social butterflies." They love to entertain and welcome people in their homes. "I" type personalities with the Gift of Hospitality openly and often express their interest in having groups or individuals over any time or for any reason. They need to be more organized and plan better. This combination can be very difficult on other family members. But their gracious hospitality is always encouraging to those who visit with them.

"D" Type Personalities With The Gift of Knowledge

Christians who are decisive and direct with quick answers to a wide range of questions often have the Gift of Knowledge. They don't hesitate to share what they know from the Bible and other subjects. They are confident and demanding. "D" type personalities with the Gift of Knowledge are more active / task-oriented with what they know. They tend to be more results-oriented, using their knowledge to accomplish tasks and more toward fulfilling a goal or impossible challenge.

"I" Type Personalities With The Gift of Knowledge

Inspiring and impressive type Christians who have a lot of Bible and various other subject knowledge often have the Gift of Knowledge. They tend to be very expressive — sometimes talk too much. They tend to have a scripture verse and answer for everything. "I" type personalities often talk a lot, but those with the Gift of Knowledge seem to have unusual knowledge over and above most other people. They are very upbeat and encouraging with their information.

"D" Type Personalities With The Gift of Leadership

Active / task-oriented Christians who like to take charge and direct groups to accomplish difficult tasks often have "D" type personalities with the Gift of Leadership. They don't take "no" for an answer. They tend to plan and push forward, challenging others to follow. They don't like sitting still and waiting for things to happen. They like to make things happen. They tend to motivate and mobilize people for accomplishing the task at hand. They like long range planning with specific short term goals that involve lots of people moving forward together.

"I" Type Personalities With The Gift of Leadership

Christians with a lot of energy and enthusiasm, who constantly rise to the top in leading others, often have "I" type personalities with the Gift of Leadership. They love to impress and inspire others to follow. They are not confrontational. They use their tremendous people skills to create exciting climates for growth. They love to be up-front. They have great verbal skills. They struggle between what people think of them and moving forward. They often come across as proud or egotistical, but are best at leading groups through their optimistic attitudes.

20

"S" Type Personalities With The Gift of Encouraging

Sensitive type Christians with the Gift of Encouraging are sweet exhorters. They share simple and slow steps-of-action to help others. They often wait for others to ask for advice. They are not pushy. They love to stabilize bad situations with practical ideas. "S"-Exhorters can be too shy. They may wait instead of aggressively confronting an issue. They need to be more assertive. Their concern for others often makes them too nice. They may need to show "tough love." "S"-Exhorters are security-oriented encouragers.

"C" Type Personalities With The Gift of Encouraging

Calculating type Christians with the Gift of Encouraging are precise exhorters. They often know just what to say. Their practical steps-of-action tend to be concise. They make competent counselors with specific insights. But they can be too hard on people. "C"-Exhorters can see what needs to be done, but fail at communicating love. They should be more sensitive to the failures of others. Having patience and kindness will increase effectiveness. They should not be so critical. "C"-Exhorters make great problem-solvers.

"S" Type Personalities With The Gift of Faith

Passive / people-oriented Christian who seem to trust God when everyone else has given up often have the Gift of Faith. They are more quiet and shy, but have an internal source of strength. "S" type Christians with the Gift of Faith are not expressive or loud about their faith. They have a steadiness and stability that makes them highly respected and sought out when it comes to increasing a group's faith. They are not pushy or bossy, but are firm and strong when in comes to believing God's Word.

"C" Type Personalities With The Gift of Faith

This is a unique combination because of the differences between the "C"s cautious and concerned behavior and the Gift of Faith's motivation to trust God no matter what. "C" type personalities with the Gift of Faith have a dichotomy of being able to trust God, while researching all the options. They prefer more information before making their final decisions, but have an unusual amount of faith, even when all the facts are not clear. They prefer in-depth research, but stand strong on the promises of God.

"S" Type Personalities With The Gift of Giving

Security-oriented type Christians with the Gift of Giving are not risk takers. They are submissive (willing) givers. They may lack the vision necessary to take on challenging projects. Sensitive to individual needs, they help others behind the scenes. They are private about giving. "S"-Givers can be too helpful. They need to guard their sincere desire to serve with a stronger determination to do what is right. They can be taken advantage of. They tend to be the most sacrificing. "S"-Givers are stable financial planners who avoid financial disasters.

"C" Type Personalities With The Gift of Giving

Compliant type Christians with the Gift of Giving are cautious. They move conservatively. They seldom make quick financial decisions. They don't like pressure. Vision and growth are often stifled because of pessimism. "C"-Givers seldom make investment mistakes, but may miss great opportunities. They need to be more positive. People often think they are critical. They should be more friendly. Respected by others, they should use their competence to help, rather than find fault. They can be valuable in financial planning.

"S" Type Personalities With The Gift of Hospitality

Christians who are more quiet and shy, but always ready and willing to have groups or individuals in their homes often have the Gift of Hospitality. They are not expressive or outgoing, but optimistic about the opportunity to help others through opening their homes to them. "S" type personalities with the Gift of Hospitality often sacrifice themselves for the sake of making others feel comfortable in their homes. They have a real servant's heart, but often have trouble saying, "no" to others.

"C" Type Personalities With The Gift of Hospitality

Cautious and calculating type Christians who love to open their homes to others often have the Gift of Hospitality. They tend to have neat homes and impress others with their cleanliness. "C" type Christians with the Gift of Hospitality like to have all the details worked out before opening their homes. They love to entertain others, even at the last minute, but always want it to be done orderly. They are thinkers and analyzers — passive / task-oriented individuals, who love to have others in their homes.

"S" Type Personalities With The Gift of Knowledge

Sweet, soft, and sensitive type believers who seem to have an unusual amount of information about so many things often have the Gift of Knowledge. They are slow to share, but when asked, have an answer for just about everything. They are more shy, than outgoing. They usually don't volunteer their knowledge, but are ready once asked. "S" type personalities with the Gift of Knowledge are faithful and loyal. They don't like hurting others and want to always help others with their knowledge.

"C" Type Personalities With The Gift of Knowledge

Christians who tend to be very careful and compliant, but exhibit tremendous Bible knowledge and are informative about various other subjects, often have "C" type personalties with the Gift of Knowledge. They love to research and understand why things are so. They love to use their knowledge of the Bible to explain things. They tend to be a little too deep for most people, but are a great resource. They often need to lighten up and learn how to be more people-oriented.

"S" Type Personalities With The Gift of Leadership

Christians who seem to be shy, but demonstrate tremendous abilities in influencing others to follow often have "S" type personalities with the Gift of Leadership. Their "S" servant type behavior seems unlikely to challenge others to follow, but they make tremendous "quiet leaders." They tend to be soft spoken and easy going. They don't like to offend anyone and work real hard at keeping everyone happy. But their sensitive leadership skills cause them to be very effective at getting groups to move out in unity.

"C" Type Personalities With The Gift of Leadership

Calculating and critical thinking type Christians, who demonstrate the unusual ability to motivate others, often have "C" type personalities with the Gift of Leadership. They go-by-the-book, researching and careful to not do anything wrong. Their influence on others to follow is often more cautious and conservative. They don't make quick or careless decisions. They plan their work and work their plan to get others involved in moving ahead. Their leadership style is more analytical and organized.

"D" Type Personalities With Gift of Showing Mercy

Determined type Christians with the Gift of Showing Mercy are rare, but dedicated to helping others feel better. Their domineering ways tend to conflict with their desire to sympathize with others. They can be decisive, while merciful and kind. "D"-Showing Mercy types are unique individuals who tend to demand that everyone display a caring spirit. Their driving personalities can be misunderstood as insensitive, while Showing Mercy is their motivation. They should guard their dominance with loving hearts. They press the need to care.

"I" Type Personalities With Gift of Showing Mercy

Inspiring type Christians with the Gift of Showing Mercy influence others to care more. They use verbal skills to generate excitement for the cause of demonstrating love. Interested in people, they induce strong feelings of concern. They can be too emotional. "I"-Showing Mercy types can over-do their influence. Some people may think their concern is all show. They like to impress others with their kindness. They need to calm down and be more humble. When it comes to evident sensitivity, "I"-Showing Mercy types are tops.

"D" Type Personalities With Gift of Pastor / Shepherd

Demanding type Christians with the Gift of Pastor/Shepherd tend to be ministry driven. Seeing the big picture, they are compelled to lead others. Their domineering ways can be misunderstood as dictatorial. They may be genuinely dedicated to shepherding others, but have strong feelings about what things should be done. Slowly working through people will make them more effective. Often taking charge, they seem to control others. Their concern for the flock is evident. "D"-Pastor/Shepherds make great visionaries.

"I" Type Personalities With Gift of Pastor / Shepherd

Inspiring type Christians with the Gift of Pastor/Shepherd are impressive. Their influence makes people enjoy working and worshiping. They can be extremely successful and must guard against pride. People look up to "I"-Pastor/Shepherds. Able to persuade, they need to be more cautious of what they promote. They love to minister and encourage others to do so. Often concerned more about what others think, they need to guard against using people to build their ministries. They can be best at using their ministry to build people.

"D" Type Personalities With The Gift of Prophecy

Demanding type Christians with the Gift of Prophecy / Perceiving are fearless concerning truth. Determined to preserve purity, they tend to dominate others. As protectors of righteousness, they proclaim truth without concern for what anyone thinks. They often feel like they have the divine right to be pushy. "D"-Prophets / Perceivers are so driving, they often offend others. They need to be more gentle, rather than always striving to expose error. They should be more sensitive to the feelings of others. "D"-Prophets / Perceivers are the most effective declarers of truth.

"I" Type Personalities With The Gift of Prophecy

Influencing type Christians with the Gift of Prophecy / Perceiving make great communicators of truth. They articulate correctness with persuasion. They tend to over-use enthusiasm and emotions to convince others. Able to induce action or reaction, they need to guard against verbal abuse. Proclaiming truth, "I"-Prophets / Perceivers should season their speech with sugar. Making great impressions, they must remember Who they represent, not what they defend. "I"-Prophets / Perceivers are inspiring protectors of the faith.

"D" Type Personalities With Serving / Ministry / Helps

Driving type Christians with the Gift of Serving / Ministry / Helps stay busy for Christ. They tend to work hard behind the scenes, doing whatever needs to be done. They can be impatient with those who don't help. Determined to minister, they tend to dominate and intimidate others to also serve. "D"-Servants are task-oriented individuals working tirelessly. They may need to slow down, relax and delegate. They can become demanding and offensive. "D"-Servants are dedicated to ministering and helping others. They are self-sacrificing doers of the Word.

"I" Type Personalities With Serving / Ministry / Helps

Inspiring type Christians with the Gift of Serving / Ministry / Helps are excited about serving. Their impressive enthusiasm makes others want to get involved. They can be too persuasive and impatient. "I"-Servants are extremely effective in inducing action. They tend to over-sell and manipulate. Influencing others, they should guard their verbal skills when the job needs to get done. "I"-Servants tend to work longer than necessary, because they talk too much. Creating an exciting atmosphere of service is their specialty.

"D" Type Personalities With The Gift of Teaching

Demanding type Christians with the Gift of Teaching are dedicated students and driving instructors. They like challenging research in order to convince others. They tend to be too forceful. "D"-Teachers make strong disciplinarians. Often domineering, they need to be more gentle with their insights. Digging deep while getting to the point can be frustrating. They should balance dedication to teaching with more people-orientation. "D"-Teachers can get the job done when it comes to explaining why something is true.

"I" Type Personalities With The Gift of Teaching

Inspiring type Christians with the Gift of Teaching are most interesting. They tell the best stories. They use clear illustrations. Their verbal skills create fascinating studies. But they tend to have lengthy classes. "I"-Teachers need to be more time-conscientious. They may also stretch the text to make a point. Concerned about what others think, they often make good impressions. They can become prideful because of their tremendous ability to communicate. "I"-Teachers are some of the most interesting instructors.

"D" Type Personalities With The Gift of Wisdom

Active / task-oriented Christians, who demonstrate unusually good judgement often have "D" type personalities with the Gift of Wisdom. They tend to be more direct and demanding with their wisdom. They often openly challenge others if they believe a decision is unwise. They have a great respect and trust in the Word of God. They need to be more loving and kind, but their decision making is often very accurate. They tend to be more confronting, not waiting for people to come to them. They make great counselors when people want straight forward and honest answers.

"I" Type Personalities With The Gift of Wisdom

Christians who get real excited about sharing their insights and concerns of right and wrong often have "I" type personalities with the Gift of Wisdom. They tend to be very expressive, talk a lot, and often demonstrate extremely good judgement. Unlike other "I" type personalities, who tend to talk a lot about nothing, those with the Gift of Wisdom show great depth of thought. They need to guard their verbal skills and learn to listen more, but when they do share, their wisdom is often surprising. They have a unique combination of articulating wisdom without sounding foolish.

22

"S" Type Personalities With Gift of Showing Mercy

Sensitive type Christians with the Gift of Showing Mercy are most loving. They are sweet servants always ready to help. They specialize in times of suffering. "S"-Showing Mercy types may be so concerned that they miss opportunities to teach lessons. They can also be fooled by insincere cries for help. They may need to be more assertive with those who use their pain as excuses. They should be more demanding. They may need to share truth, rather than always listening. When people hurt, "S"-Showing Mercy types shine.

"C" Type Personalities With Gift of Showing Mercy

Compliant type Christians with the Gift of Showing Mercy are extremely concerned about others. They see needs no one else sees. They tend to know exactly what to say. They are careful not to miss opportunities to help, but can be critical of those who don't get involved. "C"-Showers of Mercy may try to analyze why people hurt. Their conservative care is often appreciated. They need to be optimistic. Enthusiasm and inspiration are often lacking. "C"-Showers of Mercy are competent individuals who care about the sufferings of others.

"S" Type Personalities With Gift of Pastor / Shepherd

Submissive type Christians with the Gift of Pastor / Shepherd are selfless servants. They enjoy building relationships that result in ministries. They shepherd by example, not demand. They can be too nice. Often more caring than confrontational, they may need to be more assertive. Concerned about the ministry, they should be more enthusiastic. Shyness often hinders their leadership. People appreciate their interest in ministry, but some may want them to be more decisive. "S"-Pastor/Shepherds make gentle leaders.

"C" Type Personalities With Gift of Pastor / Shepherd

Conscientious type Christians with the Gift of Pastor/Shepherd are methodical. They like to go-by-the-book. They don't like to take risks and venture away from what they know works. They may need to be more open to innovation. They strive for correctness. Purity in the group is important to "C"-Pastor/Shepherds. Enthusiasm will encourage more to minister. Often conservative, they tend to be picky. Detailed assignments for everyone can often be overdone. "C"-Pastor/Shepherds are competent church leaders.

"S" Type Personalities With The Gift of Prophecy

Sensitive type Christians with the Gift of Prophecy / Perceiving are shy, but serious about truth. They seem to be soft, but their concern makes them persuaders. Motivated to proclaim truth, they tend to be gentle, but strong. "S"-Prophets / Perceivers seem to struggle with their concern for individuals and standing for correctness. This balance makes them surprisingly effective. People are often impressed when their shyness turns into firmness. They need to be careful about extremes. "S"-Prophets / Perceivers are like sleeping giants when it comes to truth.

"C" Type Personalities With The Gift of Prophecy

Calculating type Christians with the Gift of Prophecy / Perceiving are cautious and competent. They tend to be conscientious. They can be too critical of those who compromise truth. Often convincing, they tend to be confrontational. Their concern for compliance often makes them unbending. "C" Prophets / Perceivers are insightful, but can be insensitive to what others feel. They would increase effectiveness with greater interest in others, rather than always being right. As protectors of truth, "C"-Prophets / Perceivers are able to see and share correctness.

"S" Type Personalities With Serving / Ministry / Helps

Steady type Christians with the Gift of Serving / Ministry / Helps are every church's dream — the backbone of ministry. If anything needs to get done, they faithfully serve without recognition. They are not bossy, but should be more assertive. People take advantage of "S"-Servants. They should be more aggressive in seeking help. Always sensitive to the feelings of others makes them sought out. But sometimes they solve problems for those who may need to feel the pressure of their irresponsibility. "S"-Servants are the most stable servants.

"C" Type Personalities With Serving / Ministry / Helps

Competent type Christians with the Gift of Serving / Ministry / Helps are detail-oriented. They don't like loose ends. If anything needs to be done right, they are perfect for the job. "C"-Servants tend to be difficult to work with. They can be too picky. They need to be friendlier and co-operative. Often feeling like they are the only ones who ever do anything, they need to appreciate others more. Positive attitudes and enthusiasm are recommended but difficult for "C"-Servants. They can be the hardest working and compliant servants.

"S" Type Personalities With The Gift of Teaching

Stable type Christians with the Gift of Teaching are systematic researchers. They like to teach steadily, step-by-step. Their simple, but insightful instruction often lacks excitement. They need to be more animated. "S"-Teachers make faithful and loyal friends, but often resist conflict. They should strive to be more interested in results, than relationships and revelation. Concerned about harmony and accuracy, they can be too sweet and slow to share why something is true. You can count on "S"-Teachers for thorough explanations.

"C" Type Personalities With The Gift of Teaching

Compliant type Christians with the Gift of Teaching are controlled by the quest for truth. They make great researchers. Determined to discover in-depth truth, they can over-do their lessons. They can become too factual. People seem to find "C"-Teachers competent, but boring. They can lack enthusiasm and warmth. They should focus more on practical application. As critical thinkers, "C"-Teachers can sound sarcastic. When sensitive, excited and patient, "C"-Teachers make great instructors.

"S" Type Personalities With The Gift of Wisdom

Passive / people-oriented Christians with the unusual ability to make wise decisions often have "S" type personalities with the Gift of Wisdom. They are not hard and strong about most things, but do have unique insights when it comes to right and wrong. They are often sought out by others, because of their loyal and faithful way of dealing with problems. They are more quiet than most people, but when they do share their wisdom, people are often amazed. They tend to be humble and need to speak out more. But they often demonstrate wisdom that few people ever imagine.

"C" Type Personalities With The Gift of Wisdom

Cautious and slow decision-makers who also have great judgement, are often "C" type personalities with the Gift of Wisdom. They tend to be extremely analytical and sensitive to right and wrong. They are not very outgoing or expressive. They prefer to research and dig into the Bible in order to discover in-depth truth. They share their wealth of wisdom in detail with those who ask. They don't tend to volunteer their wisdom and often come across as uncaring. They should increase their enthusiasm and interest in people. They often have a lot of wisdom, but little "personality."

Involvement / Spiritual Gifts Perspective

Where your Spiritual Gifts can be used most effectively!

One of the best ways to grow as a Christian is to get involved. Identifying your natural and spiritual motivation will help. Many believers desire personal growth, but seldom find a rewarding ministry.

The following is a summary of sixteen Spiritual Gifts and how they can impact your life. Find the three Spiritual Gifts that best fit you and review what it says about those specific gifts.

PASTOR / SHEPHERDING

Abilities: Ministering to groups needing leadership.

Opportunities: Committee Chairperson, Visitation.

Warning: Don't get discouraged with those who don't follow.

Reward: Seeing the ministry improve.

Prayer: *"Dear God, Help me be patient with those who are apathetic or spiritually weak."*

ADMINISTRATION / RULING

Abilities: Organizing or delegating tasks.

Opportunities: Group Leader, Office, Personnel.

Warning: Avoid thinking everyone will get involved.

Reward: Seeing people work together to accomplish difficult tasks.

Prayer: *"Dear God, Help me to be tolerant to those who don't respond like I think they should."*

FAITH

Abilities: Unique ability to trust God and His Word for the impossible.

Opportunities: Prayer, Counseling, Finances.

Warning: Believe, as everything depends upon God, but work, as though everything depends upon you.

Reward: Influencing others to increase their faith.

Prayer: *"Dear God, Increase my faith, while I increase my work for you. Don't let me become lazy."*

PROPHECY / PROCLAIMING

Abilities: Discern right from wrong / Declare truth.

Opportunities: Community / National Concern, Finances, Steering Committee.

Warning: Don't be obnoxious or opinionated.

Reward: Helping others see the truth clearly.

Prayer: *"Dear God, Give me the sensitivity to show love, while sharing truth that may offend."*

APOSTLESHIP

Abilities: Start new churches / Pioneer new works.

Opportunities: Missions, Evangelism, Discipleship.

Warning: Be accountable to others.

Reward: Establishing new ministries that grow.

Prayer: *"Dear God, Keep my eyes on you, not on my vision. For YOU are always more important than what I do for you."*

GIVING

Abilities: Using stewardship to further God's Kingdom.

Opportunities: Finance or Planning Committee, Office.

Warning: Don't use money to control others.

Reward: Knowing you contributed to the advancement of ministry without any personal recognition.

Prayer: *"Dear God, Use my success with finances to bless the ministry and others."*

SERVING / MINISTRY / HELPS

Abilities: Serving behind the scenes.

Opportunities: Nursery, Sunday School, Ushering.

Warning: Don't become weary in well doing.

Reward: Knowing you make a difference doing what no one else may want to do.

Prayer: *"Dear God, Thank you for appreciating my labor of love, regardless of what others may fail to appreciate."*

DISCERNMENT

Abilities: Special insight concerning good and evil.

Opportunities: Counseling, Prayer, Personnel.

Warning: Guard against quick judgements.

Reward: Protecting others from poor decisions.

Prayer: *"Dear God, Give me a meek and quiet spirit, so that I can share your truth in love and not with pride."*

HOSPITALITY

Abilities: Welcoming people into their home.

Opportunities: Homeless, Encouragement, Housing.

Warning: Balance your family and personal needs with constantly inviting people to your home.

Reward: Giving others a comfortable rest and time of fellowship.

Prayer: *"Dear God, Help me to work as hard at being close to you as I do at being hospitable."*

SHOWING MERCY

Abilities: Giving sympathy and/or empathy to the hurting.

Opportunities: Hospital, Benevolence, Counseling.

Warning: Don't be a sucker to everyone.

Reward: Knowing you helped those who no one else would help.

Prayer: *"Dear God, Use me to not only help people by showing care, but also sharing truth and TOUGH LOVE when necessary."*

EVANGELISM

Abilities: Comfortably share the gospel with results.

Opportunities: Visitation, Outreach, Missions.

Warning: Don't think everyone should be as dedicated to evangelism as you are.

Reward: Leading people to Christ glorifies God.

Prayer: *"Dear God, Increase my vision for the lost, while helping me to understand why others do not share my burden."*

KNOWLEDGE

Abilities: Special ability to remember many things, especially from the Bible.

Opportunities: Counseling, Book Store, Library.

Warning: Don't get puffed up with much knowledge.

Reward: Helping others learn things they never knew.

Prayer: *"Dear God, You are the all-knowing One. May I only know and share what you want me to. Also help me not to be proud of my knowledge"*

TEACHING

Abilities: Clarify truth / Insights as to why facts are true.

Opportunities: Teaching, Training, Library.

Warning: Don't neglect other responsibilities.

Reward: Knowing people learn the truth.

Prayer: *"Dear God, Help me to be practical, not just impart truth."*

EXHORTATION

Abilities: Share practical steps of action.

Opportunities: Counseling, Crisis Center, Evangelism.

Warning: Choose words wisely.

Reward: Seeing people respond to your advice and helping them through problems.

Prayer: *"Dear God, Use me to say what you would have me to say, not what I feel at the moment."*

LEADERSHIP

Abilities: Obvious influence to motivate others.

Opportunities: Men's or Women's Ministries, Discipleship, Support Groups.

Warning: Lead by example, not just motivation.

Reward: Developing leaders to take over what you have done.

Prayer: *"Dear God, Make me a strong and sensitive leader. Help me to be a well-balanced leader!"*

WISDOM

Abilities: Special insights to make wise decisions.

Opportunities: Prayer, Counseling, Finances.

Warning: Don't become proud of your wisdom.

Reward: Helping others make good decisions.

Prayer: *"Dear God, May my wisdom always come from you and not my own judgement. Help me to always rely on your Word and not my opinions."*

Involvement / Personality Perspective

Where your personality can be used most effectively!

My highest plotting point:
Graph 1 ___ ; Graph 2 ___ ;

My next hightest plotting
points are:
Graph 1 ___ ; Graph 2 ___ .

1. First give God your "giftedness" to use for His glory.
2. Read the sections of D, I, S or C and Spiritual Gifts influences on the *Interpretation* page which correspond with your highest plotting points on your Graphs 1 & 2.
3. Look for opportunities for ministry to use your "giftedness" —
    • Search the Scriptures for insights on how God can use you.
    • Ask your minister or mature Christian friend to guide you.
4. Get involved in a ministry ASAP.
5. Pray God will control you and make you *"all things to all men."*

"D" BEHAVIOR *(Active / Task-oriented)*

Abilities: Lead, take stand, confront issue, persevere, dictate, make decisions and control.

Opportunities: Organize needed ministry, chair Stewardship Committee, head Usher's Committee, commit to specific challenge.

Warning: You want to control everyone, but must first control yourself. Remember, *"to have authority, you must be under authority."* Be loyal to your leaders.

Reward: Follow your spiritual leaders. Allow Christ to be the Lord of your life, and God will use you in a great way to move the ministry forward.

Prayer: *"Dear God, control my driving, demanding and dominant personality, so I can be a strong and peace-making leader for your glory."*

"I" BEHAVIOR *(Active / People-oriented)*

Abilities: Communicate, inspire, influence, make friends, optimism, enthusiasm.

Opportunities: Give public testimony, drama, social committee, greeter, encourager, lead discussion group and visitation.

Warning: You naturally outshine others. Don't serve purely through your *"personality."* Also, pride and sinful lusts will destroy your testimony.

Reward: God designed you to shine for Him. When you allow Him to shine through you, He will use you in greater ways than you ever imagined.

Prayer: *"Dear God, keep me humble to do your will, not mine. Help me give you and those who praise me the credit for all You have done."*

"C" BEHAVIOR *(Passive / Task-oriented)*

Abilities: Analyze, improve, discern, calculate, follow directions, do the right thing.

Opportunities: Finance Committee, long-range planning, office, record information, research, teach, organize and order curriculum.

Warning: Due to your cautiousness, criticism comes easy. Don't always be pessimistic and hard to convince. Increase your faith in God and trust those you follow.

Reward: Ministers need competent people to fulfill their visions. You can be a great blessing if you continually look at the possibilities, rather than impossibilities.

Prayer: *"Dear God, help me be optimistic in the midst of problems — a source of encouragement to those who find faith and victory difficult."*

"S" BEHAVIOR *(Passive / People-oriented)*

Abilities: Support, serve, specialize, finish what others start, work behind the scenes, do what needs to be done.

Opportunities: On call whenever needed, hospital visitation, encourage new members, office, keep records, telephoning and counseling.

Warning: Shyness hinders your opportunities to do great things for God. Be more aggressive and assertive. Be careful, people may take advantage of you.

Reward: Believing God's promise that you can do all things through Him who strengthens you, step out and try the difficult. You may be surprised what God can do.

Prayer: *"Dear God, I know you use the weak things to confound the mighty and I often don't feel capable of serving you, but through your grace I will."*

Everyone: You should never use your personality as an excuse not to do what God commands everyone to do. For example, the Bible commands you to do the work of an evangelist. **"D"**'s and **"I"**'s may feel more comfortable talking to people about Christ, while **"S"**'s and **"C"**'s may not. Yet everyone should share the *"good news."* **"S"**'s may feel more comfortable working behind the scenes, but God may call a **"S"**, like Moses, to lead a group. Or God may call an **"I"** to work behind the scenes. You must learn to *"be all things to all men that we might by all means save some."* **Whatever you do, do it through Christ. Read Galations 2:20.**

Fitly Joined Together

The following are opportunities for ministry in relationship to sixteen Spiritual Gifts. With your gifts in mind, look at all the ministries available. You should also consider many other gifts not included. You may also have various passions and interests that would cause you to fit well in a specific ministry not listed.

If you are already involved in a ministry that doesn't seem to match, don't think you shouldn't be involved. Remember Moses!

The following are just short lists of potential ministries. Your past and present experiences should also enter into your search for a good fit. Consider your spiritual gifts, personality type, interests, passions and experiences in making your choices. Add to the lists any ministries you think would also fit that gift. Once you have chosen 3 - 5 opportunities for ministry, be sure to notify your pastor, a spiritual leader, or ministry coordinator. Then get involved as soon as possible.

Administration /Ruling	Apostleship	Discernment	Encouraging	Evangelism	Faith	Giving	Hospitality
Accounting	Big Brothers	Accounting	Altar Counsel.	Altar Counseling	Altar Counseling	Accounting	Foods
Benevolence	Coaching	Counseling	Adult Choir	Big Brothers	Baptism	Benevolence	Greeters
Clerical	College / Career	Deacons	Band	Bowling	Big Brothers	Bookstore	Grounds
Construction	Construction	Discipleship	Big Brothers	Carpentry	Clerical	Clerical	Hispanic Ministry
Counseling	Deacons	Elders	Choir	Cleaning	College / Career	Coaching	Housing Visitors
Deacons	Discipleship	Finances	Coaching	Coaching	Communication	Computer	Hospital
Discipleship	Elders	Intercess. Prayer	College / Career	Communication	Communion	Construction	Hospitality
Elders	Evangelism	Newsletter	Communication	Concerts	Counseling	Curriculum	Hospice
Finances	High School	Personnel	Concerts	Construction	Curriculum	Decorating	Interpreting
Foods	Hispanic Min.	Physician	Counseling	Counseling	Deacons	Deacons	Kids Kamp/VBS
Grounds	Intercess. Prayer	Prayer	Deacons	Deacons	Discipleship	Discipleship	Kitchen
Kitchen	Jr. High	Printing	Discipleship	Discipleship	Elders	Elders	Library
Library	Long Range Plan.	Publicity	Drama	Drama	Elementary	Electrical	Meals
Long Range Plan.	Martial Arts	Records	Elders	Elders	Encouragement	EMT	Missions
Mailings	Media	Search Comm.	Encouragement	Electrical	Evangelism	Finances	Newcomers
Maintenance	Men's Ministry	Secretarial	Evangelism	Evangelism	Hispanic Min.	Floral Arrange.	Nursery
Meals	Missions	Security	High School	Foods	High School	Foods	Organ
Media	Nurse	Set-up	Jr. High	Greeters	Intercess. Prayer	Graphic Arts	Personnel
Men's Ministry	Personnel	Small Groups	Media	High School	Jr. High	Grounds	Preschool
Missions	Physician	Sound System	Men's Ministry	Housing Visitors	Media	Housing Visitors	Publicity
Newsletter	Recreation	Steering Comm.	Newsletter	Jr. High	Men's Ministry	Kitchen	Receptionist
Personnel	Script. Reader	Supplies	Nurse	Kids Kamp/VBS	Missions	Library	Script. Reader
Physician	Security	Tape Ministry	Prayer	Martial Arts	Newsletter	Long Ran. Plan.	Senior Adults
Prayer	Song Leader	Tutoring	Printing	Meals	Personnel	Mailings	Serving Meals
Printing	Search Comm.	Transportation	Receptionist	Media	Prayer	Maintenance	Set-up
Publicity	Senior Adults	Trustees	Script. Reader	Men's Ministry	Preschool	Meals	Shut-ins
Records	Single Adults	Ushers	Single Parents	Missions	Publicity	Media	Single Adults
Refugee /Hmless	Steering Comm.	Vehicles	Tape Ministry	Musician	Script. Reader	Men's Ministry	Single Parents
Search Comm.	Trustees	Video	Teaching	Newcomers	Search Comm.	Missions	Small Groups
	Visitation	Visitors Cards	Trustees	Newsletter	Senior Adults	Musician	Visitation
	Women's Min.	Writing	Video	Nurse	Single Adults	Newcomers	Weddings

Knowledge	Leadership	Mercy	Pastor / Shepherding	Prophecy	Serving / Ministry	Teaching	Wisdom
Accounting	Big Brothers	Bereaving	Altar Counsel.	Coaching	Adult Choir	Accounting	Accounting
Clerical	Coaching	Big Brothers	Baptism	Communication	Altar Counseling	Bookstore	Counseling
Counseling	College/Career	Carpentry	Big Brothers	Construction	Band	Clerical	Deacons
Deacons	Construction	Child Care	Clerical	Deacons	Baptism	Coaching	Discipleship
Discipleship	Deacons	Children	College/Career	Discipleship	Bereaving	Computer	Elders
Elders	Discipleship	Cleaning	Communication	Elders	Big Brothers	Counseling	Finances
Finances	Elders	Communion	Communion	EMT	Bookstore	Curriculum	Intercess. Prayer
Newsletter	Evangelism	Construction	Counseling	Evangelism	Bowling	Deacons	Men's Ministry
Office Machines	High School	Counseling	Curriculum	Finances	Carpentry	Discipleship	Newsletter
Orchestra	Hispanic Min.	Deacons	Deacons	Intercess. Prayer	Child Care	Elders	Personnel
Personnel	Intercess. Prayer	Discipleship	Discipleship	Kitchen	Children	Electrical	Physician
Physician	Jr. High	Elders	Elders	Long Range Plan.	Choir	Elementary	Printing
Prayer	Long Range Plan.	Elementary	Elementary	Martial Arts	Cleaning	Finances	Publicity
Printing	Martial Arts	EMT	Encouragement	Media	Clerical	Interpreting	Records
Publicity	Media	Evangelism	Evangelism	Men's Ministry	Coaching	Library	Search Comm.
Records	Men's Ministry	Foods	Hispanic Min.	Newsletter	College / Career	Men's Ministry	Secretarial
Search Comm.	Missions	Greeters	High School	Nurse	Communion	Missions	Security
Secretarial	Nurse	Homeless	Intercess. Pray.	Nursery	Concerts	Physician	Set-up
Security	Personnel	Housing Visit.	Jr. High	Personnel	Construction	Prayer	Small Groups
Set-up	Physician	Hospital	Media	Prayer	Counseling	Printing	Sound System
Small Groups	Recreation	Hospice	Men's Ministry	Printing	Decorating	Records	Steering Comm.
Sound System	Script. Reader	Infants/Toddlers	Missions	Records	Deacons	Script. Reader	Supplies
Steering Comm.	Security	Interpreting	Newsletter	Script. Reader	Discipleship	Search Comm.	Tape Ministry
Supplies	Song Leader	Intercess. Prayer	Personnel	Search Comm.	Drama	Security	Telephone Call.
Tape Ministry	Search Comm.	Kids Kamp/VBS	Prayer	Security	Elders	Steering Comm.	Tutoring
Tutoring	Senior Adults	Kitchen	Preschool	Sound System	Electrical	Tape Ministry	Transportation
Transportation	Single Adults	Meals	Publicity	Tape Ministry	Elementary	Teaching	Trustees
Trustees	Steering Comm.	Newcomers	Script. Reader	Teaching	EMT	Tutoring	Ushers
Ushers	Trustees	Nurse	Search Comm.	Trustees	Encouragement	Trustees	Vehicles
Vehicles	Visitation	Nursery	Senior Adults	Visitation	Evangelism	Video	Video
Video	Women's Min.	Organ	Single Adults	Women's Min.	Floral Arrange.	Women's Min.	Visitors Cards
Writing	Youth	Physician		Writing		Worship	Women's Min.
Yard Work	Youth Choir	Shut-ins				Writing	Writing

"Choose You This Day Who and Where You Will Serve"

The following are a few suggestions where you might "fit" best in ministry. Remember, God may lead you to do things you don't feel qualified or comfortable doing. But God always empowers you to do what He calls you to do.

There are also many challenges every Christian is called to do; such as praying, witnessing, etc. Don't let the lack of a specific spiritual gift or personality type discourage you from doing what the Bible commands. You may also feel compelled to be involved in other ministries not listed. You may even desire to be involved in ministries listed under different personality types.

"D" Types —

Carpentry	Elders	Men's Min.	Prayer	Trustees
Coaching	EMT	Missions	Recreation	Ushers
Construction	Evangelism	Long Rng Pln.	Search Comm.	Vehicles
Deacons	Finances	Personnel	Security	Worship
Discipleship	Media	Publicity	Steering Com.	Yard Work
			Teaching	Youth Ministry

"I" Types —

Band	Drama	Interpreting	Piano	Supper Club
Big Brothers	Elders	Kid Kmp/VBS	Prayer	Support Group
Bowling	Elementary	Media	Publicity	Teacher
Choir	Evangelism	Men's Min.	Script. Read.	TelephoneCall.
Coaching	Encouragemt.	Missions	Receptionist	Trustee
College/Career	Greeters	Music	Recreation	Usher
Communicatn.	Graphic Arts	Newcomers	Secretary	Video
Concerts	High School	New Mem.	Senior Adults	Visitation
Counseling	Hispanic Min.	Orchestra	Single Adults	Women's Min.
Deacons	Housing Visitr.	Organ	Song Leader	Worship
Discipleship	Jr. High	Photography	Summer Camp	Youth
				Youth Choir

"S" Types —

Altar Counselr.	Decorating	Kid Kamp/VBS	Preschool	Supplies
Baptism	Discipleship	Kitchen	Printing	Support Groups
Benevolence	Elders	Library	Records	Tape Ministry
Bereaving	Elementary	Mailings	Receptionist	Teaching
Big Brothers	Encouragemt.	Maintenance	Refug/Hmless.	Telephone Call.
Book Store	Evangelism	Meals	Scripture Read.	Tutor
Bowling	Follow-up	Missions	Search Com.	Transportation
Carpentry	Foods	Newcomers	Secretary	Trustees
Children	Grounds	New Mem.	Senior Adults	Ushers
Child Care	Hispanic Min.	Newsletter	Serving Meals	Vehicles
Cleaning	Hospital	Nurse	Set-up	Visitation
Clerical	Hospice	Nursery	Shut-ins	Visitors Cards
College/Career	Housing Visi-	Office Machn.	Single Adults	Weddings
Communion	tors	Orchestra	Small Groups	Women's Min.
Concerts	Infant/Todd.	Organ	Sound System	Worship
Counseling	Interpreting	Physician	Summer Camp	Writing
Deacons	Interc. Pray.	Piano	Supper Club	Yard Work
				Youth Choir

"C" Types —

Accounting	Discipleship	Library	Physician	Steering Com.
Band	Drama	Mailings	Piano	Tape Ministry
Benevolence	Elders	Long Rng. Pln.	Prayer	Teaching
Book Store	Electrical	Maintenance	Preschool	Transportation
Carpentry	EMT	Meals	Printing	Tutor
Children	Evangelism	Missions Mu-	Publicity	Trustee
Cleaning	Finances	sic	Records	Vehicles
Clerical	Follow-up	Newsletter	Scrip. Reader	Video
Communion	Food	Nurse	Search Com.	Visitors Cards
Computer	Floral Arrang	Nursery	Secretarial	Weddings
Concerts	Graphic Arts	Office Machin.	Security	Worship
Construction	Grounds	Orchestra	Serving Meals	Writing
Curriculum	Infants Todd.	Organ	Set-up	Yard Work
Deacons	Interpreting	Personnel	Sound System	
Decorating	Kitchen	Photography	Supplies	

Choosing where to be involved can be easy. First, pray God will give you wisdom about how your specific personality, spiritual gifts, talents, interests and experiences relate.

The Lord may also direct you to get involved in ministries that don't seem to fit your *"giftedness."* Sometimes your passions and interests create a burden to be involved in unrelated areas. God can use you in a great way as you allow Him to do His work through you.

The most practical way to discover where to serve is to consider the ministries that need your personality and spiritual gifts. For example, you may have a "S" type personality with the Gift of Serving / Ministry / Helps. Look for an opportunity to serve behind the scenes doing those things most people don't want to do — like the Kitchen or Library. You can receive deep satisfaction knowing God uses you to meet special needs.

If you're an "I" type with the Gift of Encouraging / Exhorting, you may want to get involved in a more active and aggressive outreach opportunity. "S" types prefer more passive "friendship" or *"relationship"* type evangelism or counseling.

"D" types with the Gift of Prophecy / Perceiving would serve effectively in a Community Awareness type ministry. These types prefer to perceive and declare truth.

Review all the opportunities listed with your specific personality and spiritual gift in mind. There may be other opportunities not listed. You may want to consider your talents, interests and experience. For example, you may not have an "I" personality with the Gift of Showing Mercy, but you have a burden to win the lost. Your passion and experience will mean you fit well in an evangelism ministry.

Be sure to communicate with the appropriate ministry leader. Notify him or her about your personality type, spiritual gifts, talents, interests and experience. Ask for counsel concerning where others may think you fit best. Scripture teaches, *"In the multitude of counsel there's safety."* Temporarily volunteer to serve in various ministries. Notice how you fit and feel as you serve. Be sensitive to how the Holy Spirit uses your involvement to help others and bless you.

Choose 3 - 5 *"Opportunities For Ministry"* To Consider:

_____

_____

_____

_____

_____

Leadership Insights

Most everyone responds to life's challenges and choices according to his or her personality.
Therefore, individuals who relate to others must be *personality wise*.

For example, High "S" leaders should not engage High "D" followers in small talk. "D"s prefer leaders who get-to-the-point. They want "bottom line" answers. They respond best to those who are not going to waste their time.

On the other hand, High "S" followers feel comfortable with leaders who are systematic, slower, and steady in their approaches. "S"s don't like fast talking, quick pace responses. "S"s respond best to stable and sensitive leaders.

Leader Styles

The following describes different leadership styles. People tend to lead according to their personalties, rather than adapt to the styles of others.

"D" Leaders —
"D"s are *take control* and *be in charge* types. They don't like people telling them what to do. "D" leaders can be too pushy and forceful. They need to control their direct and demanding approach to management. They make better leaders when they learn to slow down, be gentle, and not so demanding of others.

"I" Leaders —
"I"s are inspiring and enthusiastic. They love to lead and influence others. Naturally great presenters, they tend to talk too much. "I" leaders need to listen more and not be so sensitive to rejection. They are the most impressive and positive leaders. "I"s love crowds, but need to be interested in individuals.

"S" Leaders —
"S"s are the sweet, steady and stable leaders. They seldom demand anything. They are friendly and loyal, but tend to be too nice. They need to be more aggressive and assertive. Overly sensitive to their shortcomings, "S"s need to be more confident. They hate to take risks. They often miss opportunities because of their caution. Reliable and relaxed, they are more reserved.

"C" Leaders —
"C"s are competent and compliant. They go by the book and want to do everything just right. They are thorough and detail-oriented, but tend to be too informative. "C"s need to be more positive and enthusiastic. They answer questions people aren't asking. When optimistic, "C"s are extremely influential. They should not concentrate on problems, but focus on potentials.

The most effective Leader is the blended Servant Leader. These type individuals learn how to adapt and become "all things to all men." They understand that everyone is often motivated by their specific personality. They guard their strengths from overuses, and improve/perfect (2 Corinthians 12:9-10) their "uniquenesses / weaknesses."

Follower Styles

People also follow according to their personalities. Identifying individual followers' styles make leaders more effective.

"D" Followers —
"D"s respect strong leaders. They want to be part of a winning team. They follow with power and authority in mind. They wonder, "*Will this action make me more respected and / or get the job done?*" "D" followers need choices, rather than "*get-in or get-out*" ultimatums. They need opportunities to do their own thing.

"I" Followers —
"I"s follow with their hearts. They tend to be impulsive followers. They want opportunities that will make them look good. "I" followers talk a lot. They make great first impressions. Their high egos and ability to persuade often turn them into the leaders in order to rise to the top. Sometimes you don't know who's leading whom.

"S" Followers —
"S" followers don't make quick decisions. They like leaders who are understanding and gentle. They want to establish a relationship with a leader who will be around for a long time. "S"s are concerned about service and stability. When it comes to sensible and slow judgment, "S" followers feel right at home. They like familiar and low-key environments.

"C" Followers —
"C"s are "Consumer Report" type followers. They analyze each decision. They love research and development. "C"s are quality oriented followers. They don't like quick or costly decisions. Picky and precise, they follow with their minds, rather than hearts. "C"s seldom respond positively at first. They often want time to think about their decisions. Once convinced, they follow best.

Blended Servant Leaders allow the Holy Spirit to control their drives, passions, and wills in order to motivate others more wisely. Servant Leaders are Transformational Leaders who raise people up to follow on a higher plain. Anyone can be a Servant Leader. Your giftedness and "DISC" personality type is not most important. It's your relationship with God and others that makes the difference. ***God doesn't always call the qualified, but He always qualifies the called!***

How To Handle Conflicts

Often, the greatest hindrances to healthy relationships are personality conflicts. Positive individuals, desiring to build good relationships, are often discouraged because of misunderstandings and clashes with others.

This section is designed to help you discover why people do what they do under pressure and why you may conflict with others. Life's success principles on how to handle clashes are clear. The problem is many people are not aware of their "*sensitive spots.*" Everyone needs to learn more about avoiding and resolving conflicts.

Every personality has its "*hot button.*" Everyone can act like a "D" when pushed too far. The following are tendencies of personalities as they relate under pressure.

Review the following pages with your Behavioral Blends in mind. Read each section to see how you may respond as a specific personality type. Also consider how you may respond differently because of your "hot and cold buttons."

To improve your effectiveness, control your personality and never use it as an excuse for poor behavior!

Remember — *Most problems today are not theological— they're relational — personality conflicts and clashes with others.*

"D" Behavior and all Spiritual Gifts

Under Pressure:
Becomes dictatorial, domineering, demanding, angry, intense, forceful, direct, bossy.

Sources of Irritation:
Weakness, indecisiveness, laziness
Lack of — discipline, plan, purpose, direction, authority, control, challenge.

Needs To:
Back off, seek peace, relax, think before reacting, control self, be — patient, loving, friendly, loyal, kind, sensitive.

"I" Behavior and all Spiritual Gifts

Under Pressure:
Becomes hyper, overly optimistic, immature, emotional, irrational, silly, wordy, selfish.

Sources of Irritation:
Disinterest, slowness, pessimism, details, time restraints, antagonism, doubt, structure, lack of — enthusiasm, team participation.

Needs To:
Listen, count the cost, control emotions, be — humble, strong, disciplined, punctual, careful with words, conscientious.

"C" Behavior and all Spiritual Gifts

Under Pressure:
Becomes moody, critical, contemplative, negative, worrisome.

Sources of Irritation:
Incompetence, disorganization, foolishness, dishonesty, inaccuracy, wastefulness, inconsistency, blind faith, false impressions.

Needs To:
Loosen up, communicate, be — joyful, positive, tolerant, compromising, open, trusting, enthusiastic.

"S" Behavior and all Spiritual Gifts

Under Pressure:
Becomes subservient, insecure, fearful, weak-willed, withdrawn, sympathizer, sucker.

Sources of Irritation:
Pushiness, instability, inflexibility, anger, disloyalty, insensitivity, pride, discrimination, unfairness.

Needs To:
Be — strong, courageous, challenging, aggressive, assertive, confrontational, enthusiastic, outgoing, expressive, cautious, bold.

Natural Responses To Conflict —
"D"s — Want To Attack
"I"s — Want To Expose Others
"S"s — Want To Support or Submit
"C"s — Want To Criticize

Recommended Wise Responses —
"D"s — Restore With Love
"I"s — Make others look good
"S"s — Care Enough To Confront
"C"s — Examine Own Self First

Spiritual Gifts & Conflicts

One of the most, if not **THE** greatest hindrance to spiritual growth is conflict. Excited Christians, desiring to serve God, are often discouraged because of misunderstandings and clashes with other Christians.

This section is designed to help you discover why Christians often do what they do under pressure. It may explain why you may conflict with others. Scripture is clear on how to handle clashes. The problem is many Christians are not aware of their "motivations." Even Spiritual Gifts can be overused and abusive. The best thing about you can become the worst.

Allow God, not your feelings, to control your gift/s.

Gift of Evangelism —
Under Pressure:
Becomes hyper, talkative, doesn't listen well, pushy, intense, forceful, direct, bossy.
Sources of Irritation:
Apathy, indecision, laziness, all talk and no go, Lack of — concern for the lost, inactivity, purpose, direction, leaders as examples, challenge.
Needs To:
Back off, slow down, relax, minister to needs of others, build relationships, be — patient, loving, friendly, kind, sensitive.

Gifts of Prophecy and / or Apostleship —
Under Pressure:
Becomes dictatorial, domineering, demanding, angry, intense, forceful, direct, bossy.
Sources of Irritation:
Weakness, indecisiveness, laziness.
Lack of — discipline, plan, purpose, direction, authority, control, challenge.
Needs To:
Back off, seek peace, relax, think before reacting, control self, be — patient, loving, friendly, loyal, kind, sensitive.

Gifts of Teaching, Discernment and/or Knowledge —
Under Pressure:
Becomes too serious, haughty, high-minded, critical, contemplative, judgmental, moody, analytical.
Sources of Irritation:
Shallowness, inaccuracies, disorganization;
Lack of — preparation, validation, plan, direction, authority, control, depth.
Needs To:
Relax, build relationships, ask more questions, allow for discussion, spend more time being practical, be — more friendly, funny, upbeat, enthusiastic.

Gifts of Exhorting and / or Faith —
Under Pressure:
Becomes hyper, overly optimistic, immature, emotional, irrational, silly, wordy, selfish.
Sources of Irritation:
Disinterest, slowness, pessimism, details, time restraints, antagonism, doubt, structure, lack of — enthusiasm, team participation.
Needs To:
Listen, count the cost, control emotions, be — humble, strong, disciplined, punctual, careful with words, conscientious.

Gift of Pastor / Shepherding —
Under Pressure:
Becomes serious, insensitive, overly concerned, nosey, intense, regimented, overbearing.
Sources of Irritation:
Spiritual weakness, indecisiveness, immaturity;
Lack of — discipline, plan, vision, direction, power, control, consistency.
Needs To:
Serve by example, build relationships, relax, think before reacting, control self, be — patient, loving, kind, considerate, tolerant.

Gift of Showing Mercy —
Under Pressure:
Becomes subservient, insecure, fearful, weak-willed, withdrawn, sympathizer, sucker.
Sources of Irritation:
Pushiness, instability, inflexibility, anger, disloyalty, insensitivity, pride, discrimination, unfairness.
Needs To:
Be — strong, courageous, challenging, aggressive, assertive, confrontational, enthusiastic, outgoing, expressive, cautious, bold.

Gifts of Serving / Ministry and / or Hospitality —
Under Pressure:
Becomes selfless, sacrificing, weak-willed, cooperative, sympathetic, sensitive.
Sources of Irritation:
Inconsiderateness, inactivity, anger, disloyalty, Lack of—volunteers, help, concern.
Needs To:
Be — Challenging, aggressive, assertive, bold, enthusiastic, expressive, delegating, creative, confident, leading.

Gifts of Giving and / or Wisdom—
Under Pressure:
Becomes picky, judgmental, sensitive, intense, manipulative, vulnerable.
Sources of Irritation:
Waste, stinginess, insensitivity; Lack of — discipline, willpower, direction, determination, Lack of— stewardship, control, challenge, concern.
Needs To:
Be — more flexible, patient, risky, understanding, forgiving, not taken advantage of.

Gifts of Administration/Ruling and/or Leadership—
Under Pressure:
Becomes moody, critical, contemplative, negative, worrisome.
Sources of Irritation:
Incompetence, disorganization, foolishness, dishonesty, inaccuracy, wastefulness, inconsistency, blind faith, false impressions.
Needs To:
Loosen up, communicate, be — joyful, positive, tolerant, compromising, open, trusting, enthusiastic.

Biblical Resolution Management

Covenant —

In obedience to God's Holy Word and commitment to practicing Biblical Resolution Management, I promise to follow the Principle of Priorities. That is, my priorities are to glorify God, build harmony in the church, and avoid conflict. I will do as Matthew 18 admonishes—go to an offending brother "first alone."

First Step —

I will not first share the offense with another person. I am committed to restoring the relationship, rather than exposing possible sin. I recognize most problems with people are personality clashes, and I will try to understand their actions based upon their perspective.

Second Step —

If going to a person "first alone" does not resolve our differences, I promise to seek a neutral and mature individual who will listen to each of our perspectives of the problem. This person will hopefully be able to shed light on one or both of our blind spots or areas of needed growth in order to glorify God.

I recognize that the "witness" may reveal or say things I won't like, but I will believe God is using him or her to resolve the conflict, rather than take sides. (The "witness" must be an individual with deep spiritual wisdom and highly respected by all those involved.)

Warning —

I will not seek to find others who have also been offended, nor share my concerns with potential "witnesses" prior to the meeting with my "offending brother." The purpose of having a "witness" is not to validate my hurt but rather to open my heart and mind to the possible needs I may have regarding my relationship with others.

I realize my friends may naturally listen to my concerns, but also take up my offense. I will, therefore, not cause them to become a party to a possible division and disharmony because of our friendship. Whenever I feel an urge to share the offense with my friends, I will pray and commune with God about my hurt.

Confronting Ministry Leaders —

I believe in the scriptural admonition to not rebuke an Elder (spiritual leader), other than in grave matters of misconduct and open sin (1 Timothy 5:19). I will earnestly pray for and follow those God has placed in leadership over me. I will not allow anyone to criticize them without following the principles in Matthew 18 and without the specific person present.

If I have a problem with my ministry leader, I will go "first alone" to them. I will not share my concern with anyone. I will listen and try to understand their perspective of the problem. If I am not satisfied with their explanation and continue to have animosity, I will ask their permission and counsel to find a "witness" who will listen to our conflict.

If the "witness" finds I have misunderstood the situation and should continue no further, I will trust God to complete His work in my life by casting my burden on the Lord and leaving it there. If the "witness" agrees with my concern and finds the ministry leader wrong and the leader refuses to hear the "witness," we will then find a group of two or three other "witnesses" who will hear the matter and determine what God is doing through this conflict.

Serious Step —

If I continue to find fault with a ministry leader and cannot worship in "spirit and truth," I will seek to join another ministry rather than cause any conflict and disharmony. I am committed to pleasing God through resolving my conflicts, even if it means separating myself from the source of my irritations.

Ultimate Goal —

I commit myself to be spiritual rather than "normal" and supernatural rather than "natural" when it comes to solving my problems with others. I want God's will and way to resolve my conflicts and will do as the Holy Bible teaches, regardless of my normal and natural feelings.

My ultimate goal is to glorify God through bearing much fruit, getting involved in ministry, and avoiding and resolving conflicts.

Joy & Giftedness

The words "joy" and "gifts" are related in the Bible. They both come from the same Greek root word . Their connection has wonderful implications — real joy comes when we exercise our gifts. God divinely designed us with plan and purpose. His purpose was to bless us, by our discovering and using our giftedness for His glory.

Discovering our giftedness is fascinating. But the main thing is to keep the main thing the main thing! What is the main thing? It is to "*glorify God with your body and spirit,*" 1 Corinthians 6:19,20. We glorify God most, while reaping the benefits of true joy when we allow God to use us as He designed us.

Scripture admonishes us to "*present our bodies, living sacrifices to God . . . to discover what is that good and acceptable will of God,*" Romans 12:1,2. If you really want to discover God's will for your life, you must give God your giftedness. Give Him your feelings, thoughts, and actions, both naturally with your personality and supernaturally with your spiritual gifts.

The Bible teaches us not to be like children tossed to and fro, all mixed up in life. Instead we should "*speak the truth in love that we may grow up in Christ,*" Ephesians 4:15.

We all need to mature in Christ, so we can enjoy life as God intended!

Because these lessons are so important, your church has provided you with this tremendous learning experience, Everything would be wasted if you ended this study without determining to be involved in a specific ministry. Also learn how to avoid and resolve conflicts based upon Biblical Resolution Management principles and ministry will be more meaningful.

Consider making a commitment to follow Christ. Dedicate your giftedness to God. He wants to bless you more than you could ever imagine. Remember happiness is a choice. You will experience true joy, "*charis,*" when you are exercising your giftedness. But you must make a commitment to exercise your giftedness.

Don't wait for anyone to ask you to get involved. Start this week by just showing up and saying, "*I'm ready to serve!*" Don't be surprised if things are a little disorganized and chaotic at times. Remember the Day of Pentecost was one of the most confusing, but glorious days of all!

Exercise your giftedness to experience joy!

All these insights should help you understand where you fit best in ministry. *Remember, every member is a minister!* This could be your Day of Pentecost, when God pours out His blessings on your life and uses you in ways you never dreamed. But it could also be a nightmare, because of *people*. Serve God, regardless of whatever conflicts and clashes you may have, and you WILL be blessed.

Keep your eyes on Christ and you will succeed!

Opportunities For Ministry

You should complete this page once you understand better what your spiritual gifts and personality types are.

Everybody is somebody in His Body! Every Christian should be involved in a ministry. Service encourages spiritual growth. You will mature as a Christian while you exercise your giftedness. You can experience tremendous joy as you minister to others.

Not only do you need to serve, the church also needs servants. Nearly every ministry often lacks people who will give of themselves to help others. Believers should donate their time, talents, and treasures as Stewards (managers) of God's work.

Both you and the church will benefit when every member becomes a minister. The following are suggestions where you may "fit" best in serving the Lord. Completing all the questionnaires and this survey is part of discovering your **SHAPE** for ministry.

Rick Warren has popularized the emphasis on discovering your

SHAPE — "S" for spiritual gifts, "H" for heart (passion), "A" for abilities (talents), "P" for personalities, and "E" for experience. These letters identify the ministries that make up your **SHAPE.**

Prayerfully review each opportunity below, keeping in mind your spiritual gifts, personality type, and passion. Place an **"E"** next to each area in which you have experience. Place an **"I"** in the areas you find interesting or have abilities in. Place an **"H"** in the areas where you have a heart or passion (where you are most excited) about that ministry.

Then choose 3 specific opportunities where you want to serve. Share the choices with your minister or a leader who can give you wise counsel. Ask them to help you find a special place of ministry where you can exercise your giftedness.

There are many other opportunities of ministry not listed. You may even want to start a new one. *Grow For It!*

1. ___ Accounting
2. ___ Adult Choir
3. ___ Altar Counselor
4. ___ Band
5. ___ Baptism
6. ___ Benevolence
7. ___ Bereavement
8. ___ Big Brothers
9. ___ Bookstore
10. ___ Bowling
11. ___ Carpentry
12. ___ Child Care
13. ___ Children
14. ___ Choir
15. ___ Cleaning
16. ___ Clerical
17. ___ Coaching
18. ___ College / Career
19. ___ Communication
20. ___ Communion
21. ___ Computer
22. ___ Concerts
23. ___ Construction
24. ___ Counseling
25. ___ Curriculum
26. ___ Decorating
27. ___ Deacons
28. ___ Discipleship
29. ___ Drama
30. ___ Elders
31. ___ Electrical
Elementary
    32. ___ Sunday
    33. ___ Mid-week
    34. ___ Special Events
35. ___ EMT
36. ___ Encouragement
37. ___ Evangelism
38. ___ Finances

39. ___ Floral Arrangements
40. ___ Follow-up
41. ___ Foods
42. ___ Graphic Arts
43. ___ Greeters
44. ___ Grounds
45. ___ Hispanic Ministry
High School
    46. ___ Sunday
    47. ___ Mid-week
    48. ___ Special Events
49. ___ Housing Visitor
50. ___ Hospitals
51. ___ Hospitality
52. ___ Hospice
Infants / Toddlers
    53. ___ Sunday
    54. ___ Mid-week
    55. ___ Special Events
56. ___ Interpreting for the Deaf
57. ___ Intercessory Prayer
Jr. High
    58. ___ Sunday
    59. ___ Mid-week
    60. ___ Special Events
61. ___ Kid's Kamp / VBS
62. ___ Kitchen
63. ___ Library
64. ___ Long Range Planning
65. ___ Mailings
66. ___ Maintenance
67. ___ Martial Arts
68. ___ Meals
69. ___ Media
70. ___ Men's Ministries
71. ___ Men's Softball
72. ___ Men's Basketball
73. ___ Missions
74. ___ Musician

75. ___ Newcomers
76. ___ New Members
77. ___ Newsletter
78. ___ Nurse
79. ___ Nursery
80. ___ Office Machines
81. ___ Orchestra
82. ___ Organ
83. ___ Personnel
84. ___ Photography
85. ___ Physician
86. ___ Piano
87. ___ Prayer
Preschool
    88. ___ Sunday
    89. ___ Mid-week
    90. ___ Special Events
91. ___ Printing
92. ___ Publicity
93. ___ Records
94. ___ Receptionist
95. ___ Recreation
96. ___ Refugee/Homeless Min.
97. ___ Scripture Reader
98. ___ Search Committee
99. ___ Secretarial
100. ___ Security
101. ___ Senior Adults
102. ___ Serving Meals
103. ___ Set-up
104. ___ Shut-Ins
105. ___ Single Adults
106. ___ Single Parents
107. ___ Small Groups
108. ___ Song Leading
109. ___ Sound System
110. ___ Steering
111. ___ Summer Camp
112. ___ Supplies

113. ___ Supper Club
114. ___ Support Groups
115. ___ Tape Ministry
116. ___ Teaching
117. ___ Telephone Calling
118. ___ Tutoring
119. ___ Transportation
120. ___ Trustees
121. ___ Ushers
122. ___ Vehicles
123. ___ Video
124. ___ Visitation
125. ___ Visitor Cards
126. ___ Weddings
127. ___ Women's Ministries
128. ___ Women's Softball
129. ___ Worship Leader
130. ___ Writing
131. ___ Yard Work
132. ___ Youth
133. ___ Youth Choir

My Graph 1 Behavioral Blend:

(i.e.) S/C or D/C _____

My Graph 2 Behavioral Blend:

(i.e.) S/C or D/C _____

My three highest Spiritual Gifts:

_____
_____
_____

My three greatest Passions are:

_____
_____
_____

Name _____ Home Phone _____

Address _____ City _____ State _____ Zip _____

I would possibly like to serve in these ministries: (1) _____; (2) _____; (3) _____

33

Biographical Survey

This information is designed to simply help your church or ministry know more effectively how to serve you. Please give as much of the following information as possible.

Please Print

Name: _____ Email _____

Address: _____

City: _____ State: _____ Zip: _____

Home Phone: _____; Gender: Male _____; Female _____

Date of Birth: _____; Current age: _____; How long have you been a Christian: _____.

Employer: _____; Position: _____

Work Phone: _____; How long employed there: _____

Marital Status: ____ Married; ____ Single; ____ Divorced; ____ Separated; ____ Widowed. How long status: _____

Spouse's Name: _____

Number of Children: _____; Ages: _____; _____; _____; _____; _____.

Spouse's Employer: _____; Position _____

Date Joined Church: _____; Position in Church: _____

Sunday School Class: _____;

How would you describe your spiritual maturity: Weak ___; average ___; above average ___; good ___; strong ___.

Church attendance Frequency: ___ Almost always; ___ Often; ___ Seldom; ___ Never.

 My three highest Spiritual Gifts are:

(1) _____; (2) _____; (3) _____

My personality type in Graph 1 is: _____; My personality type in Graph 2 is: _____

My greatest passions are:

(1) _____; (2) _____; (3) _____

I would like to possibly serve in these following ministries:

_____; _____; _____.

❏ I also promise to try and follow Biblical Resolution Management principles.

Spiritual Gifts Numerical Ratings Chart Totals on page 5 in your profile booklet.

A	B	C	D	E	F	G	H	I	J	K	L	M	N	O	P

Transfer the totals from your "Total Boxes" on page 10 to the specific Total Boxes below.

❻ TOTAL BOXES

	D	I	S	C	B	
"M"						= 24

	D	I	S	C	B	
"L"						= 24

Be sure to first complete the *Spiritual Gifts Graph*, your *Personality Two Graphs*, and *Opportunities For Ministry Survey*. Complete this page, then tear it out, and give it to your minister or group leader.